DAVID,

MAY GOD BLESS YOU ON YOUR LIFE'S JOURNEY

Chris

SEVEN WORDS FOR THE END OF YOUR JOURNEY

A Guide for Dying Well Based on Jesus's Seven Words of the Cross

CHRISTIAN C. SPOOR

Author photo by Paul S. Robinson Photography

WestBow Press books may be ordered through booksellers or by contacting:

WestBow Press
A Division of Thomas Nelson & Zondervan
1663 Liberty Drive
Bloomington, IN 47403
www.westbowpress.com
1 (866) 928-1240

ISBN: 978-1-5127-7645-4 (sc)
ISBN: 978-1-5127-7646-1 (hc)
ISBN: 978-1-5127-7644-7 (e)

Library of Congress Control Number: 2017902634

Print information available on the last page.

WestBow Press rev. date: 02/27/2017

CONTENTS

DEDICATION

Dedicated to the memory of the people

I have been able to serve

at the end of their earthly journeys,

and to their family members and friends

who loved and cared for them.

EPIGRAPH

Therefore we do not lose heart. Though outwardly we are wasting away, yet inwardly we are being renewed day by day. For our light and momentary troubles are achieving for us an eternal glory that far outweighs them all. So we fix our eyes not on what is seen, but on what is unseen, since what is seen is temporary, but what is unseen is eternal.

—2 Corinthians 4:16–18

ACKNOWLEDGMENTS

As my long-time marriage partner, Trudy has enabled me to spend countless hours at all times of day and night with parishioners and patients in their time of need. Then when it came to writing this book, she constantly encouraged me, shared insights, and in many readings of the manuscript suggested needed improvements. Her love and support made this book possible. Thank you, Trudy.

Thanks also to my daughter, Mary (an astute reader and positive literary critic), for going through many versions of the manuscript. And thanks to my sons—Mike, Jeff, and Ron—for urging me on and saying kind words about this writing project.

My gratitude to Terry Wynne for her enthusiastic encouragement, and to Marcia Glass, who helped with the fine points of grammar and punctuation.

It has been great working with my literary agent, Melanie Jongsma of Lifelines Publishing. I deeply appreciate her professional guidance in preparing the manuscript for publication and her assistance in making people aware that it is available.

Most of all, I express gratitude and love to my Savior Jesus, whose own example, experience, and wisdom constitute the inspiration and content of this book.

PREFACE

While serving as pastor of Living Springs Community Church in the greater Chicago area, I participated for eighteen years in the annual Good Friday service sponsored by the South Suburban Ministerial Association. Each year this ecumenical service consisted of seven meditations by area clergy. There were seven because on Good Friday, the day Jesus was crucified, he spoke seven sayings that are recorded in the biblical accounts of his dying. They are called the "seven words of the cross." Much has been written about these seven words. In keeping with the voluminous literature on the subject, our meditations generally consisted of mining theological and devotional messages from the words of Jesus. There is indeed profound meaning in these words, and exploring this meaning can inspire the faithful to deeper devotion.

Without detracting from any of this, I have come to realize that the seven words also have another layer of meaning that is not often recognized. This became clear to me when, following my retirement from congregational ministry, I served for six years as chaplain with Peace Hospice in Chicago. My area of ministry then became focused on serving the terminally ill and their families. That is when I began to realize how the seven words spoken by Jesus as he was dying not only give theological insight for devotional life but also are especially applicable to people who are facing death, and also to their loved ones. In his dying, Jesus experienced and expressed what, sooner or later, we all must encounter.

I write this book as a follower of Jesus. From that perspective, I believe that dying can be a drawing closer to God and a joyful preparation for the life to come. I hope that in reading this book you will find that, though it says a lot about dying, it is really about life. The Bible says that in Jesus there is life. I believe that, and through faith in him I love life and strive not to fear death. How I will in fact deal with death when my time comes I do not know. But I do know that, like everyone else, I will die someday. And I know that Jesus, who teaches me how to live, also teaches me how to die. That is what the seven words of the cross are about.

Christian Spoor

INTRODUCTION

Dying is not easy. It can be filled with fear, regrets, loneliness, and pain. But Jesus's seven words offer guidance and hope for the end of our earthly journey.

The purpose of this book is to help people die a good death. That term sounds incongruous, just like Good Friday—how can that Friday when Jesus suffered a horrible death be called good? Both *good death* and *Good Friday* convey confidence that in a very bad situation, good can prevail.

The seven words deal with the real needs and experiences of dying people. It may be easy for a healthy person to tell the dying what to expect. But Jesus did not lecture from a distance. He entered into the experience, speaking for the dying as he himself was dying. Just as throughout his life Jesus taught people how to live, so in his dying he taught us how to die. Of all the end-of-life resources available, there is nothing more practical than the seven words of the cross.

The seven words are not just for the elderly. Jesus himself was in his thirties when he died. Earlier, during his teaching ministry, he had cautioned people to always be ready because things can happen when you least expect them. A wise application of the seven words is to live by them at all times so that when we come to the end of our journey, we may be prepared.

Before we get into the seven words, let us look at how Jesus himself faced the reality of his impending death. During the last months of his earthly life, Jesus recognized that he was in constant danger. The opposition to his teaching had become so great that it was only a matter of time till he would be assassinated. He also knew it was his destiny not to fight it or run from it. So he faced it, and knowing how devastating his death would be to his disciples, he sought to prepare them for it. The disciples of Jesus did not respond well to this because they believed that Jesus was the Messiah. Indeed, to them much of what Jesus did and said appeared to indicate that he was the Messiah. Except ... his talking about the fact that he would have to suffer and die. This is not what his followers wanted to hear. They wanted to share in his messianic glory for the rest of their lives. And they were well aware that some Old Testament passages predicted that the Messiah would live a long life (see Psalm 91:16, 21:4).

Is not that what we all want—long life? Forget about death conversations! But thoughts and conversations about death do not need to be morbid. From the words of Jesus, we can learn how to focus our thoughts and actions on positive outcomes even at the time leading up to death. During my service as a hospice chaplain, I learned how important it is to face facts. For many people, the dying process is harder than it needs to be because they and their families and friends are caught in webs of denial to the very end. Jesus's disciples did not want to hear him talk about dying, so they failed to support him in his final hours of anguish. So also in our time we may find that family, friends, and even clergy do not dare to use the D word for fear of discouraging the patient. Too often, when a terminally ill person has attained the courage to accept that he is dying, others will try hard to push him into denial: "Don't say that; you can still live a long time." Or: "You've got to have faith; just believe that you are going to get better." Or: "You have to keep fighting." But if we let others push us into an illusion, we miss out on the power of faith that can give us peace—and even joy—when we come to the end.

How can we face death with serenity and hope? I believe Jesus's seven words of the cross can be a great help to all who face their mortality, and also to those who care for them. In these words, we hear how Jesus in his final hours still cared for the needs of others, laid bare his inner self by speaking of his own anguish, and showed how faith will triumph in the end.

FIRST WORD

Forgive

When they came to the place called the Skull, they crucified him there, along with the criminals—one on his right, the other on his left. Jesus said, "Father, forgive them, for they do not know what they are doing." (Luke 23:33–34)

It is fitting that the first word of the cross should be *forgive.* During his three short teaching years, Jesus said much about forgiveness. He was very emphatic about it. He never just suggested that forgiveness might be a good option. He taught that forgiving is essential in our relationship with people and with God. And so, at the end of his earthly journey, under terrible circumstances, he practiced what he had preached—he prayed a prayer of forgiveness.

"Father, forgive them, for they do not know what they are doing." Forgive them? Forgive whom? There were many people who had done wrong to Jesus. Just before his crucifixion, within a period of about twelve hours, Jesus had been betrayed by one of his disciples, repudiated by another, and abandoned by the rest. He had been arrested without cause by the temple police, and he was physically abused during his interrogation at the hands of religious and civil authorities. King Herod and his thugs had mocked and ridiculed Jesus. A bloodthirsty crowd of people had demanded his death. The Roman governor, knowing Jesus to be innocent of the charges brought against him, had nevertheless condemned him to death. Soldiers of the local garrison had pressed a wreath of thorns on his head and flogged him mercilessly. And then the final agony—he was nailed to a cross and subjected to another round of mockery from the bystanders.

To all this Jesus responded: "Father, forgive them!"

Did Jesus ask forgiveness for the betrayer, the denier, the disciples, the temple police, the Sanhedrin, the mocking crowd, the king, the governor, or the soldiers? He did not specify. We may therefore assume that Jesus cast his net of forgiveness wide enough to include all. And yes, now, two thousand years after Calvary, we can be confident that Jesus's forgiving prayer also included you and me.

Forgiveness: The Primary Work of Jesus

It is recorded in Luke 5:17–25 that one day some friends brought their paralyzed buddy to Jesus for healing. Jesus did not respond by immediately taking care of the medical problem. To the surprise of everyone present and the consternation of some, Jesus simply said, "Friend, your sins are forgiven." This was not what the sick man or his friends had asked for. Nevertheless, to Jesus this was a priority. His first gift to the man was forgiveness—freely given.

There were bystanders who were offended by this. They objected that Jesus had no authority to pass out forgiveness just like that. "Only God can do that," they said. But Jesus checkmated them by then healing the man's paralysis—proof that he had God-given authority to forgive sins as well as to heal.

Forgiveness was at the heart of Jesus's ministry. For that purpose he lived and died and was raised again from death. This gift of Jesus is as relevant for us as it was for the people of his time. Whatever struggles and burdens you have, do believe that Jesus's forgiveness prayer was also for you.

Throughout his ministry, Jesus shared his remarkable insight of the kingdom of God with anybody who would listen. He taught in the temple, in village synagogues, in homes, in fields, and at the lakeside. People were astonished at his teachings—particularly at the authority that exuded from him. Even in our time his teachings are treasured by millions and still totally relevant. As we seek to live by them, we gain insight, courage, and strength for everyday living. As we practice what he taught, we make life better for everyone around us.

Just as for three years Jesus taught us how to live, so on the last day of his life he taught us how to die. The seven words of the cross enable us to deal with the stresses and fears of dying, and they guide us to face the end of life in a spirit of faith and hope.

What Is Forgiveness?

So what about this first word of the cross—*forgive*? It is a word of love, comfort, and encouragement to us since we are aware of our failings. The first word also challenges us to look at our inner feelings about other people and our relationships to them. Do we still carry resentments against those who have wronged us? And do our consciences remind us of times when we ourselves have wronged others and never tried to make it right? From the lips of the dying Jesus, we are given the urgent reminder to bring forgiveness into play while there is still time.

What is forgiveness? It begins by seeking to soften hurt and anger into a more peaceful inner state so that we are willing to give the offender freedom from retribution and humiliation. Forgiveness then enables all involved to go forward without being emotionally shackled to past injuries. Thus, forgiveness leaves the wrong behind on a road where there are no U-turns.

Forgiveness Has Two Dimensions

Jesus is the preeminent teacher of forgiveness; he practiced it, and the religion that is built on his teachings is based on forgiveness. Jesus taught that forgiveness has two dimensions: our relationship to God and our relationships to other people. These two dimensions are inseparably linked.

First then, we must acknowledge that as fallible human beings, we have done wrong to God and to people. We must acknowledge that we are in need of forgiveness. Second, we must let go of anger and resentment against people who have done any form of wrong to us. We must be willing to put closure to past hurts and to create an environment in which people who were in conflict can now be at peace with each other. Think of how the world would be different if forgiveness were universally practiced!

In her book *Is Reality Secular?* Mary Poplin writes:

> Forgiveness is perhaps the single most significant psychological principle in the Judeo-Christian approach to psychological health.

> Forgiveness is a two pronged principle—people receive forgiveness from God for things they do or fail to do, and people forgive others unconditionally for the same.

> Until I opened my life to Christ, I, like the general secular academic community, absolutely hated the idea of sin; even hearing the word sin was like scratching nails on a board, and hearing the name Jesus was even more disconcerting. Now I see that the solution to sin—the simple acknowledgement of sin for what it is and seeking God's forgiveness and cleansing—is one of the most brilliant, hopeful and freeing principles of Judeo-Christianity.[1]

Forgiveness can bring closure and healing to very painful memories. It also prepares us to meet our Maker. Jesus taught that at the end of life, we all must face the final judgment, and if we have not forgiven those who wronged us, how can we expect mercy for ourselves (Matthew 6:14–15)? Facing the end of life is a final opportunity to forgive others and to ask others to forgive us. This may not be an easy thing to do. Forgiveness can be complicated—and it is good to be aware of the complexities. But when all is said and done, it comes down to one simple thing: no matter how deep the pain, and

[1] Mary Poplin, *Is Reality Secular?* (Downers Grove, IL: Intervarsity Press, 2014), 139, 146.

no matter how undeserving and obstinate the other person, we really must forgive. And let us do it as Jesus did—casting the net of forgiveness wide and making no exceptions.

The Limits We Put on Forgiving

But is that really so? Must we forgive everyone who has wronged us? This is a huge challenge, and because it can be so difficult, people often want to set limits on forgiveness. The famous example is Peter, who asked Jesus, "How many times shall I forgive my brother or sister?" (Matthew 18:21). When asking this, Peter suggested that seven times would be a pretty generous limit. After all, wouldn't people take advantage of us if we kept forgiving on and on?

But Jesus's answer was clear: "Not seven times, but seventy-seven times." In other words, stop counting; just do it.

Another way we try to limit forgiveness is to expect that, as a condition of our forgiving, the other person must first apologize and ask for forgiveness. But clearly that is not what Jesus waited for when he spoke of forgiveness. Not one of the people who had hurt and abused him had expressed remorse. Yet he said, "Father forgive them." In fact, by adding "for they do not know what they are doing," he recognized that none of them even thought they had done wrong to him.

So what do we do if the offender does not ask for forgiveness? Perhaps she does not recognize the harm she has caused, or the offender is too proud to say, "I am sorry," or she thinks you ought to just get over it. In that case we still can forgive, for in the act of forgiving we free ourselves from the chains of resentment. Yes, we will have to accept that the relationship may remain strained without full reconciliation.

There is a difference between forgiveness and reconciliation. Reconciliation includes (1) recognition of wrongdoing, (2) confession, and (3) forgiveness. This takes two people, whereas forgiveness requires only one. It is sad when the other person does not do her part. In that case there is no reconciliation—but don't let that keep you from forgiving. You cannot control what the other person will do with it. But do unburden yourself from the hurt and anger. Since the other person has not acknowledged wrongdoing, it will be harder to forgive. But it can be done, and you will benefit by doing it.

The best way to do this is to follow Jesus's example. Make it a prayer, and say of those who have wronged us, "Father, forgive them, for they do not understand the hurt they have caused."

Another limit we put on forgiveness relates to the size of the offense. Someone might say, "I am a forgiving person, but there are some things I cannot and will not forgive." Let us recognize that there are indeed offenses that are extremely painful—rape, murder, causing financial ruin, and many others. It is one thing to forgive a careless driver who caused a fender bender. How much bigger will be the hurt and anger against a drunk driver who caused an accident that killed or permanently disabled someone we love? The fender bender can be quickly forgiven, especially when the insurance company pays for the damages. But in the other case, we face a mass of shock, pain, grief, anger, indescribable loss, and broken hopes and dreams.

In order to forgive a great wrong like this, we will have to draw on our deepest spiritual and emotional resources. In this situation, forgiveness will be a process. It will involve mourning, coping with pain, dealing with disorientation in our daily activities, struggling with faith and anger against God, and learning to live in a new reality that is permanently marred by great loss and grief. We will need to recognize that it is virtually impossible to do this in our own strength. Reaching out to supportive family and friends or talking with a counselor or pastor can be helpful. But ultimately this is the time to cry out to God for help and to pray that Jesus will share with us his spirit of forgiveness. Somewhere in this convoluted process, the time comes when we can begin to think of the offender with the goal of forgiving.

Forgiveness: It is Personal, Not Theoretical

Is forgiveness then for everyone, without exception? Inevitably discussions about this come around to Hitler or Stalin or some other human monster—surely people like that have done too much evil to be forgiven! The problem with this kind of discussion is that it does not help us with our own issues. It sidetracks us from the forgiveness we need for ourselves, and the forgiveness we have to extend to others. Jesus, always the down-to-earth, practical teacher, might say something like, "Forget speculations about other sinners. Leave them to God. All you are asked to do is to deal with people and situations in your own personal experience."

That is what the first word of the cross is about. It is not a theoretical discussion about the ethics of forgiveness; it is a very personal thing. That is what it was for Jesus; it came out of his own immediate experience of horrible hatred from his enemies and desertion by his friends.

The Burden of Confession

Granted that we ought to forgive everyone who has wronged us, what about confession? Does every sin we have committed need to be confessed? Confession certainly is a healing thing for the one who makes the confession, but let us also be aware that confession can place a heavy burden on the person being confessed to.

The case of Chuck and Evelyn comes to mind. Chuck had committed adultery. His wife, Evelyn, never found out. Many years later, Chuck decided he should confess to Evelyn and ask her forgiveness. She was shocked and deeply hurt by what he had done and by the fact that he had kept her in the dark for so many years. She also felt unfairly imposed on by Chuck's implication that she should immediately be ready to forgive him. Would it, after all these years, have been kinder to Evelyn if Chuck had carried his secret to the grave?

There is no easy answer. For one thing, even while it was hidden from Evelyn, at least one other person knew about it. What if someone told Evelyn after Chuck's death? She would then be left with the painful feeling that years of marriage had really been, on Chuck's part, a relationship of deceit. On the other hand, what had Chuck achieved by his confession? He had deeply hurt his wife and placed the burden of resolution (forgiveness) on her. So what would have been the loving thing to do: confess or leave it closed?

My thought is that it would have been better if Chuck had first confessed to God and then sought counsel from someone else, such as a pastor, a wise and trusted friend, or a professional counselor. They might have suggested to him that he should break it to Evelyn gently by opening his heart and letting her know how he had been burdened by guilt. He should in no way have implied that now the ball was in her court and she was under obligation to forgive him.

He should have assured her that he understood her pain and could only hope that in time she could come to forgive him.

Forgiving and Remembering

What about forgetting? People say, "Forgive and forget." The fact is, there is no delete key in our memory. We can forgive, but we cannot forget. Nor does the Bible teach that we must forget. There is, however, a world of difference between remembering after we have forgiven and remembering when we have not forgiven. When we have forgiven, the rough edges of our memories will be softened, our anger will be tempered, and we may actually be able to wish and pray for the wellbeing of the one who has hurt us. Without forgiveness, the memory will fester and bind us to a painful past.

How do we forgive when we are no longer in contact with the offender? We live in a mobile society. People move away. When we are ill, relatives and friends from across the country may not be able to visit us. It is even more painful when a relative or friend living two blocks away cannot get himself to come see us. People may consciously or subconsciously avoid us when there are sensitive issues between us. So, how do we forgive those who are not present? Here again the example of Jesus is pertinent. In the twelve hours prior to his death, literally hundreds of people had taken part in abusing him in one way or another. Only a limited number of these were present at Calvary when he prayed, "Father, forgive them." Yet we can reasonably assume that his prayer includes the ones present as well as those not present.

The God Factor

The important point is that Jesus prayed that God would forgive them. When people harm each other, they not only do wrong to another human being, but they also sin against God. Therefore, for people to be freed from guilt, forgiveness needs to operate at two levels. We must forgive each other, and we also need to be forgiven by God. In this world offenders may "get away with it." But there will be a final accounting on judgment day. Jesus taught that in the end nothing will be covered up; it will all come out in the open (Luke 8:17). The question is, what do we want to happen to those who have wronged us? Do we take grim comfort in knowing they will get their due? Or can we rise to the level of grace and ask that God will be merciful to them?

This leads us to realize that forgiveness is free, but it is not cheap. The profound meaning of Jesus's crucifixion is that he died for the sin of the world. His was no ordinary death. He was the Son of God choosing to be the sacrificial Lamb of God, who takes away the sin of the world (John 1:29). There is a real transaction that took place when Jesus died at Calvary. He was not just saying the word *forgive*. He was paying the bill for all the ways we have messed up. Accept that because of him you can be forgiven and your record will be expunged. And since he paid the price for all human sin, let us not keep others and ourselves in bondage to our anger. By the love of Jesus, let us forgive and set free those who have hurt us.

Forgiveness and Guilt

People often keep struggling with guilt after they have asked for forgiveness. They will say, "I have asked forgiveness, but I do not feel forgiven." And so they keep praying again and again for forgiveness. At that point someone might advise them that they should learn to forgive themselves. This advice is undoubtedly well meant, but can it produce the freedom from guilt we seek?

In the Bible, there is no instruction for people to forgive themselves. Forgiving oneself is also not part of historic Christian teaching. When we continue to struggle with guilt, and when we keep on blaming ourselves for past mistakes, the solution is not that we need to forgive ourselves. What we really need to do is to accept and assimilate the fact that God has forgiven us and that therefore we truly are guiltless in God's sight. That is what really matters.

Believe that God is ready and eager to forgive. Similarly, when we forgive others, God will authenticate that act. That is what God does, freely and ungrudgingly. Let us not leave God out of the loop of forgiveness. Jesus shows us that in this first word of the cross. He did not say, "I forgive you all," but he prayed, "Father, forgive them." Of course, included in this prayer is the fact that he himself forgave, but in his forgiving he brought his heavenly Father into the picture.

When I was a pastor, a woman came to me and confessed a sin she had committed years ago. She told me that every day for fifteen years she had asked God's forgiveness, but she continued to feel guilty. We spent time talking about God's forgiveness—it is freely given to us because of the atoning death of Jesus, so we do not need to keep begging forgiveness over and over again. I suggested to her that just as a wound will not heal if we keep scratching it, so we will not find peace if we keep stirring up something that God has already forgiven. We agreed that she would think about this for one week and then come back. We would then pray only once more for forgiveness, with the commitment that after that she would never again pray to God about it. This was a big step for her, but she made the commitment. A week later we both got on our knees, and she prayed for the final time about this matter. Then together we thanked God that she had been forgiven. She later told me that this was the moment she was freed from her guilt.

The Power of Forgiveness

When Jesus was crucified, he was flanked by two condemned criminals. Both of these hardened men joined the hostile crowd in mocking Jesus. But after a while, one of them changed his tune. He came to an amazing insight that Jesus was about to enter the heavenly kingdom. He said, "Jesus, remember me when you come into your kingdom" (Luke 23:42). What brought about this remarkable change? I am inclined to think that it happened when he heard Jesus praying for forgiveness for his enemies. For a man who had lived a hard life of crime, forgiveness was a new language. He himself had mocked Jesus, and now he recognized that Jesus's prayer of forgiveness also included him. Forgiveness is a powerful agent of change. It infuses God's grace into a calloused world of hurt and division. Forgiveness is life-giving. It set a dying convict onto the road to paradise.

Only one of the two criminals responded that way. The other's heart was untouched by the word of forgiveness. This is still the way of things today. For some people, forgiveness is the word of healing and restoration. But others may reject forgiveness and the freedom it brings.

How people respond is out of our hands. Don't let that discourage you. Forgive anyway. When you forgive, you perform one of the greatest acts of love—just as Jesus did.

Prayer

Father in heaven, I thank you that you are the God of love who freely forgives. Because you are my loving God, I ask you to forgive my sins against you and against others. And as I have prayed for forgiveness, I ask that you will now set me free from all feelings of guilt and self-accusation. Help me also as I forgive all those who have in any way hurt or offended me. Please keep me focused on Jesus, who in his living and in his dying demonstrated the true meaning of forgiveness. In his name I pray. Amen.

SECOND WORD

Paradise

Two other men, both criminals, were also led out with him to be executed. When they came to the place called the Skull, they crucified him there, along with the criminals—one on his right, the other on his left. … One of the criminals who hung there hurled insults at him: "Aren't you the Messiah? Save yourself and us!" But the other criminal rebuked him. "Don't you fear God," he said, "since you are under the same sentence? We are punished justly, for we are getting what our deeds deserve. But this man has done nothing wrong." Then he said, "Jesus, remember me when you come into your kingdom." Jesus answered him, "Truly I tell you, today you will be with me in paradise." (Luke 23:32–33, 39–43)

Thoughts of the future are always with us. We make educational choices based on the kind of life we want to live in years to come. We schedule appointments, anticipate vacations, hope for a promotion, check the weather forecast, plan a wedding months before it happens, and count the months until we make the last payment on the car. I myself am a hobby gardener, and gardeners, like farmers, are always dreaming of how next year's crop will be even better than this year's.

But all these plans are contingent—they may or may not come true. Only one thing is sure for every living person: in one way or another, we will all come to the end of our earthly lives.

Usually we don't think about this much because it seems a long way off, and it is not pleasant to think about anyway. But there comes a time when thoughts about the end of life and the hereafter take on a new urgency for us—such as when the doctor diagnoses a serious illness and tells us the prognosis is not good, or when we get older and our bodies remind us in various ways that our remaining time is getting shorter.

"What Do I Believe?"

As we begin to think seriously about the end of life, it is likely that we will reflect on what we have believed about a life hereafter. Some of us were raised by parents who believed in heaven and passed that faith on to us. We learned about it in Sunday school, and when Grandma died, we were told not to be sad because she had gone to be with Jesus in heaven. Others were raised in a worldview that this is the one and only life you get, and when you die, there is nothing more. As adults we may have departed from what we were taught in childhood, working out our own set of values as we encountered new ideas and cultural attitudes. Today's intellectual climate is oriented toward physical reality—things that can be observed, tested, and explained—and people have doubts about an unseen reality that is supposed to last forever.

These values and beliefs may make a big difference in how we deal with the end of life. Of course, we may choose to ignore the issue. Or we may face up to it, in which case we may find ourselves torn between hope and doubt, wondering to ourselves, "Is it really so? Am I about to disappear into nothingness? Or is there an existence with eternal happiness waiting for me?" Confronting our mortality brings us face to face with the ultimate question about reality and the meaning of life.

Facing Death

The second word of the cross can help us negotiate these hopes, fears, beliefs, and doubts about the life hereafter. It is unique among the seven words of the cross in that it is the only one that involves a dialogue. But this is no armchair dialogue. It is a question and promise exchanged between two men who are subjected to unbearable suffering and who know without a doubt that they are about to die. This is no time for idle questions or superficial, feel-good answers. This is the moment of truth.

Two executions were scheduled in Jerusalem for that day. Both were for convicted criminals whose names have been lost to history. At the last moment, a third was added—Jesus. He had just been condemned and was immediately added to the death list of the day. There would be no time allowed for appeal.

There was a lot of notoriety about Jesus. He was the most talked-about man in Jerusalem. So they gave him the center spot at Calvary, with a criminal crucified on each side of him. The Romans crucified people in public places along well-traveled roads. One reason was that public display of the victims' suffering might be a deterrent to further crime. Another reason for crucifying in public was to attract a crowd to mock the condemned. True to purpose, the crowd of Good Friday did their jeering, especially at the one who was the famous miracle-worker. At first (as recorded in Matthew 27:44) the two criminals, though themselves suffering the awful crucifixion pains, also taunted Jesus. But then a remarkable change came over one of them. No longer mocking, he began to see a new reality.

As noted in the previous chapter, he likely was deeply touched by Jesus praying for forgiveness for his enemies. Having observed how Jesus forgave and prayed for his enemies, the criminal could no longer mock. He saw in Jesus a demonstration of love that he had not known before. As a result, having no one else to turn to, he put his faith in Jesus. Yes, it took a lot of faith to observe Jesus—bloodied, naked, and mocked—and to believe that this dying human wreck would soon enter his kingdom.

Anticipating the Kingdom

How did this criminal ever get the idea that Jesus was about to come into a kingdom? When Jesus was crucified, there was a notice nailed to his cross that read: "Jesus of Nazareth, the King of the Jews" (John 19:19). Governor Pilate had ordered it as a way of irritating the Jewish leaders. For the crowd watching the crucifixion, this notice became another reason to ridicule Jesus: "Ha, look what you get for pretending to be King Messiah!" The mocking bystanders were not the only ones to see the notice. If the crosses were arranged in somewhat of a semicircle (as often portrayed in art), the convicts also could read the notice. In fact, one of them threw a bitter challenge at Jesus: "If you are the Christ, save yourself and us." For the other the sign became a further incentive to stop mocking and start believing. He saw the sign—"King." It brought to mind things he had heard. One could hardly live in Judea of that time without having heard about that strange miracle healer/prophet who spoke about the kingdom of heaven. For this convict, the dots connected, and with the clarity of vision that sometimes comes to the dying, he was the first to understand that Jesus's kingdom is not of this world. "Jesus," he begged, "remember me when you come to your kingdom."

Jesus's response was not a casual, "Sure I will," the kind of promise we make and soon forget. Jesus was clear and specific: You can count on it—today you will be with me in paradise. In other words, yes, there is a life hereafter, and it is beautiful.

That is what paradise is—a place of beauty. Think of a garden with lush green vegetation, streams of pure water, exquisite flowers, and no pain, no hatred, no mocking, everything in harmony. It is the Garden of Eden renewed. It is the realm where Jesus will be King.

From the Skull to the Garden

It is remarkable that from the horrible place of crucifixion Jesus should speak of a place called Paradise. The crucifixions were done on a small hill called *Golgotha* in Aramaic or *Calvary* in Latin. Both words mean the same thing—Skull. Why was this hill called the Skull? Opinions differ on this. Some say that this barren little hill got its name because it looked like a skull. Others say that because it was a place of frequent executions, there were always unburied skulls lying about.

Either way, it was known as the Skull—the place and symbol of death. And Jesus knew that from this awful Skull place, he and his neighbor were about to enter the renewed Garden of Eden. They were going from this horrible place of death straight into the eternal kingdom of life. There was in Jesus's mind no doubt about the life to come. He knew the way. Paradise was ahead.

Can you believe there really is such a place? When we come to the point where we know that our days on earth are limited, faith becomes more important than ever. However, faith will be challenged, and we may ask if all that talk about the life hereafter is really true. When we are overwhelmed, depressed, and feeling defeated, we may say, "I just can't believe it." As we will see in the fourth word, Jesus also had his spiritual struggle—but that was about a different issue. As far as life hereafter is concerned, he never wavered. He was sure of it—sure that both he and his fellow sufferer were going there that very day.

Assurance

I received a phone call from my dear friend Alice (not her real name), who lived half a continent away. Three years earlier Alice had been diagnosed with cancer. Medical treatment had brought remission for two and a half years. Then the disease came back with a vengeance. It was declared incurable. That last call from her came three days before her death. Without chitchat, Alice came directly to the point: "Chris, I am dying. You have been my friend and my pastor, so be honest with me. Do you believe without a doubt that there is a life hereafter?"

A question like that left no room for platitudes or insincere answers. Only honest truth would do. I replied, "Alice, I do believe it, yet, sometimes I have my doubts."

"Then what do you do with your doubts?" she replied.

"When I doubt, I think of Jesus. He spoke with complete conviction of heaven. He said that he came from the Father in heaven and was going back to the Father. I believe Jesus was not a liar and that he knew what he was talking about. I decided long ago that I would not live my life by my doubts, but by the word of Jesus."

"Thank you," she said. "That means a lot. I will do it."

There are many opinions about life after death. Each person has her or his own opinion. But what do we really know for sure? It may be hard to believe in heaven; but it is equally hard not to believe. We just do not have empirical evidence for or against either view. But we do have the word of Jesus—that he came from that other realm; that through his unique relationship with God, his Father, he was in constant touch with that realm; and that he was going there to prepare a place for others.

The Same, But Different

As his earthly life came to a close, he once again affirmed, with the second word of the cross, that there is a life to come, and it will be beautiful. What can we know about that life? Jesus's post-Easter resurrection appearances give us a fascinating hint. He was the same, yet he was radically different. He could materialize and disappear before the eyes of his disciples, and he could apparently move through solid doors and walls. This suggests that the life to come is lived in a different dimension than the universe in which we now live. In the light of current theories of physics, that is not farfetched.

The sameness and yet radical difference of the life hereafter indicate that the various biblical descriptions of the world to come are metaphors, not to be taken literally. Golden streets, pearly gates, river of life, New Jerusalem, the Father's house with many rooms, and paradise are all symbolic descriptions that give us a feel for something that is good beyond words. Other biblical descriptions tell of a place where there is no evil, no sorrow, no pain, and perfect peace among the innumerable multitude of every race and nation, all experiencing the overwhelming presence of God.

Preparing for Paradise

How can our dying be shaped by the second word of the cross? First of all, as you face death, latch on to this word of Jesus:

"You will be with me in paradise." Say and repeat to yourself, "I am going with Jesus to paradise." If you wonder whether you have been a good enough person to merit this, remember that Jesus spoke the second word to a man who by no means had been good enough. It is not a question of whether we have been good enough. It is about the love of God who "so loved the world that he gave his one and only Son, that whoever believes in him shall not perish but have eternal life" (John 3:16).

Don't let doubt and fear darken the end of your life on earth. Have faith. Have faith in Jesus. Jesus was the most remarkable human being who ever lived. He said that he is the way and the truth and the life and that only by him we can come to God (see John 14:6). If at times you experience fear and doubt, latch on to the words of Jesus. He can be trusted.

Sometimes people say that it does not seem fair that this criminal (who, as far as we can tell, had lived a godless life) should enter heaven hand in hand with Jesus. I can't speak for Jesus, but I think he would probably say something like, "Don't spend your time thinking about what is fair. Rather, be happy that with God it is never too late to turn your life around." That seems to be the point of a story that Jesus once told about day laborers who worked a long, hard day getting the same pay as those who were hired at the last hour (Matthew 20:1–16). The significance of this story is that even if you did not come to faith earlier in life, you can still turn to God at the end of the day, and Jesus will welcome you. The playing field will be level for everyone. It was not too late for the criminal on the cross; it is not too late for you.

Hope for the Living

There is an additional way in which the second word can shape our dying: we can give comfort and encouragement to other people. Our dying is not just about us. Those who love us (spouse, parents, children, grandchildren, siblings, friends, medical caregivers) are also in pain. As they see us declining, they are already experiencing what is called anticipatory grief. It may well be that the last earthly task the dying can complete is to strengthen and comfort their loved ones. That is what Jesus did. Though he was in searing physical pain himself, and though he was the object of scorn and mocking, he gave comfort and hope to the man next to him.

Do you still have the presence of mind and the energy to speak words of hope and comfort to your loved ones? If so, do it. If you have faith, share that faith with them. In many relationships there is so much reticence to talk about the inner things of spiritual life. Often spouses don't even know what goes on inside their partner's heart and mind. Parents may have given their children a religious upbringing without ever talking about their own spiritual journey. Regardless of how open or closed you have been about your inner beliefs, you can still leave a spiritual legacy. Let your loved ones know of your faith and hope and anticipation of paradise. Assure them that you know where you are going. Speak of your hope of seeing them again. Encourage them to always walk in faith.

For my wife, Trudy, and me, our greatest desire is that our descendants to the end of time will walk in the way of Jesus. We have told our children and grandchildren that, and if God gives me clarity of mind when I am dying, I want to once again let them know that this is my hope and testament of faith.

However, many deaths do not allow for that kind of sharing at the end of life. A person may be comatose or intubated and therefore not able to speak, or heavily sedated because of pain. There is also the mental death of dementia long before the body dies. All of these make conversation at the very end impossible. Therefore, if we want to leave a spiritual legacy, we should not wait to the end. The kind of conversations that can be so meaningful at the end of life can be equally significant at an earlier stage. The very realization that we are all mortal challenges us to be more transparent about our inner life all along the journey.

Prayer

Jesus, you have been where I am now. And my hope is to be going where you are. If there comes a time when I doubt, remind me and assure me through your Holy Spirit that heaven is for real and that you are there to welcome me. Take away my fear of dying. Give me joy in anticipating my entrance into paradise. I also pray that my family and friends may find hope and comfort in knowing there is life with you beyond the here and now. Amen.

THIRD WORD

Loved Ones

When Jesus saw his mother there, and the disciple whom he loved standing nearby, he said to her, "Woman, here is your son," and to the disciple, "Here is your mother." From that time on, this disciple took her into his home. (John 19:26–27)

The funeral was over. The pastor had spoken comforting words. At the end of the graveside service, friends and relatives had once again offered expressions of sympathy. Then the funeral home's limo had dropped off the widow and her three young children at their home. For the bereaved wife, it had all passed as in a daze. Now, as she entered her familiar home, reality struck her hard. She stood rooted to the floor in her kitchen, and after a long silence, she said, "What do I do now?" Her children never forgot the despair of those words.

A week before, life had been so normal. Then her husband developed a high fever, and three days later, he died. He had worked at a laboring job. His modest paycheck was their only income. For the widow and her children, there was no pension, no life insurance, and no savings. She had no marketable job skills. She faced a bleak future.

The passing of a loved one, whether expected or suddenly, is not just a matter of emotional bereavement. It can involve many losses—financial disaster, social isolation, and the loss of someone you depended on. There are also the innumerable things that have to be taken care of—responsibilities that one was never prepared for.

During a terminal illness, friends and family will give a lot of attention to the patient. They make attempts to encourage and comfort, or even entertain and distract. This is good, but we must not forget the needs of the friends and family members who experience anticipatory grief during the patient's illness, and who face even greater burdens after the loved one passes. Jesus's third word from the cross reminds us to stop and think of others, even as he did. His mother, Mary, and his friend John were the two people who had been closest to Jesus. Now, at Calvary, they were present in deep anguish as they watched him die. In spite of his own suffering, Jesus did not neglect their needs. His words to them show us his concern for the challenges he knew they would face after his death.

Seeing Others' Pain

Since before Jesus was born, Mary had known that her son would be a very special person. An angel had told her that her child would be called the Son of the Most High and that he would reign over an everlasting kingdom (Luke 1:32–33). She also remembered the unusual events in Bethlehem the night her baby was born: angels from heaven announced peace on earth, and shepherds came to adore the newborn baby. Surely, her son was destined for great things!

During Jesus's youth, Mary took note of her son's extraordinary spiritual maturity. When he became a man, she saw the amazing power of his ministry. She marveled at his radical teaching about how to live in the kingdom of God. Perhaps as a mother she wondered at times if he was being too radical for his own good. But to the end she believed in him and loved him with all her mother's heart. Imagine her anguish and crisis of faith when she saw her beloved son tortured, defiled, and nailed to the cross. How could this fit in with what the angel had announced about her son being God's chosen Messiah?

Standing heartbroken at the foot of the cross, Mary may have recalled the time when she and Joseph had taken the infant Jesus to the temple to be dedicated. There they had encountered a stranger who predicted that because of this child, "a sword will pierce your own soul" (Luke 2:35). Now she experienced the fulfillment of that prophecy. But how did it all fit together—the promised glory and the predicted pain?

Also among the very small groups of Jesus's followers who were present at Calvary was John, a young man who loved Jesus dearly. It is believed that John was the youngest among the twelve disciples of Jesus, probably no older than in his late teens. He had eagerly accepted Jesus's invitation to become a disciple. He learned well; more than anyone else, John caught the essence of Jesus's teaching—that love is the most important thing. John had such great hopes for Jesus! He was ready to follow him for the rest of his life, and now his hopes were crushed as he saw his dear Master dying an accursed death.

Now, in the midst of his own suffering, Jesus is very aware of the suffering of John and Mary. His love takes action, and he draws them together with the third word of the cross.

Caring for Mary

It is often assumed that with these words Jesus was providing material security for his mother by asking John to take care of her. This makes some sense because Mary was likely a widow. The last reference to her husband Joseph was twenty-two years earlier when Jesus was a boy of twelve. After that, Joseph dropped out of the story—hence the assumption that he had died. In Bible times life was not easy for widows. There was not much room in that culture for an independent woman to earn a living for herself. Most widows depended on charity.

Still, there is the question of why Jesus would ask John to take care of Mary. What about other members of Mary's family? The Bible records that Jesus had "brothers." (Note: according to Roman Catholic teachings they would have been either his cousins or sons of Joseph by an earlier marriage. Nevertheless, whether they were sons, stepsons, or nephews, they would have been Mary's nearest family.) Could they not have taken care of Mary? One would think so if the need was strictly material. But quite possibly her need was more comprehensive.

Caring for John

It is significant that Jesus's concern goes both ways—from Mary to John and from John to Mary. While Mary the widow may have had material needs, this cannot be said of John. He was a healthy young man. He had a trade. His father owned a fishing business. He even had connections among influential people in Jerusalem. He certainly could take care of himself financially. In terms of material needs, John and Mary were in different leagues, and there was nothing Mary could do for John.

What they had in common was emotional devastation. Of all people they were the closest to Jesus. Their bereavement was the greatest. Mary with the sword-pierced soul, whose faith in the promise of God for her special son, was now in tatters. And John, for whom Jesus was his hero, now also found his dreams shattered. Mary and John were in deep grief, and they both needed each other to lean on. In his dying moments Jesus thought of them and urged them to be there for each other.

With the third word of the cross Jesus teaches that the grief of Calvary was not only about him, but there was also the grief of his bereaved family and friends. And so the third word teaches the dying to be mindful of others who are also facing loss and deep grief. The death of a loved one usually results in multiple losses for the survivors. The losses they are facing will certainly be emotional, but often also material. With the third word Jesus teaches us the importance of providing for those who will survive us.

Listing the Losses

How can those who are facing the end of life also be mindful of the pain of the ones they will leave behind? To recognize the magnitude of the losses that are part of bereavement, it will be helpful to list some of them. Let us consider what the losses of the bereaved may be.

Financial losses. The widow referred to in the beginning of this chapter faced a bleak future of financial hardship. How, by the grace of God, she was provided for is another story. But the fact is that someone's death can result in economic hardship for the surviving spouse, children, or other family members. The most immediate need may be the cost of a funeral and accumulated medical bills. Another immediate impact may be loss of wages—what was a two-income family has now suddenly become a one-income household. If the deceased was retired, pension benefits may end, and social security income of the surviving spouse will decrease. The deceased may have been the owner of a small business that provided income for the family. But now with the owner/entrepreneur gone, the surviving family members may be unable to continue operating the business. In the case of a family with small children, the surviving spouse may now be faced with childcare expenses. Death, just as a divorce, can have many financial implications—most of them negative.

Loss of companionship. There may be many things you used to do together—traveling, going to church, watching the game, seeing a movie, playing bridge at the club, sharing experiences, making joint decisions, making plans. Now that is gone. And wherever the road ahead leads you, your companion will not be there with you. Worst of all is the empty house during the long days and dark nights. It is not enjoyable to be alone. You so miss the companionship, the fun times, the jokes, the laughter, and the emotional security.

Loss of help. The burdens of bereavement include many practical, everyday things of life. A widow in a bereavement support group said, "I did not know how much I would miss my handyman." Others in the group quickly added to the list, relating how they missed the household cook, the grocery shopper, the one who remembered birthdays and anniversaries, the one who looked after getting the car fixed, the one who took care of finances and the maze of medical insurances, or the partner in raising the children. Suddenly one has to take on all the responsibilities that were shared by two.

The grief of children. When children lose a close family member or friend, they often suffer alone. They do not know how to talk about their pain, and many adults do not know how to talk to bereaved children. And so the children are left alone in their bewilderment. Death of a dear one often is for children also a crisis of faith. A child may have prayed for mother's healing and with the pure faith of a child expected that God would answer, "Yes!" What now? Again, the child will likely internalize his or her crisis of faith even though this is when communication, understanding, love, and comfort are most needed.

Loss of purpose. This happens particularly to caregivers, especially when death is preceded by a long illness or a long period of decline due to age. Other family may have lived far away or just found it convenient to "let Sue take care of Grandma." This primary caregiver (who almost always is a woman) will have given much of herself. She may have sacrificed a career or education or her possibility for romance. She has poured her life into being a caregiver. When the loved one dies, she feels that she has lost her purpose for living.

Loss after a dysfunctional relationship. It is hard enough to lose someone when the relationship was good—at least then there can be comfort in the cherished memories. But when the relationship was broken, abusive, or just wearying, there are additional grief burdens. There may be conflicted feelings of relief and sadness, of anger and regret for what could have been. If other people know that the relationship was not good, they may say the wrong thing, like, "It must be a relief that he is gone." That may be partially true, but it hurts more than it comforts when others say it. It is also particularly hard to hear people eulogizing the departed in glowing terms when you know he was not at all a nice person.

Things We Can Do

As Jesus was sensitive to the needs of his mother and his friend, how can we be sensitive to the material and emotional needs of those who will mourn our passing? Following is a list of some of the things we can do to make the loss easier for our loved ones.

1. *Have a will, and make sure it is up to date.* It is wise not to put this off until one is actually in the last stage of life. We all need to face the fact that we are mortal! No one knows at the beginning of a day whether this day may be the last one of our earthly life or whether we still have many years to live. If you made a will years ago, things may have changed. Beneficiaries may have died, and new people may have become important in your life. Your assets and charitable interests may also have changed. Wills need to be reviewed from time to time and updated if necessary. If you have minor children, it is also very important to designate who will raise the children if both parents die. A will is not just a tool to pass on assets. It can help avoid squabbles among family members about who gets what. Don't just assume this will not happen in your family. People in grief do not always function rationally and lovingly. Finally, having made a will, make sure people know where it is.

2. *Let your faith be known.* When we talk about making a will or last testament, we generally are talking about the disposition of our financial/material assets. But those are not the only things of value that we leave behind. What about our values and beliefs? These will constitute our most important legacy. (Actually, these are the things we have been passing on to others all

along in our daily lives.) It is a beautiful thing when we intentionally leave a testament of faith. It is a statement (spoken or written) of what our innermost beliefs are. Let others know about your faith in God, your relationship to Jesus, and your hope of eternal life. If you have never clarified matters of faith in your own life, do it now. You can do no better than to be guided by John 3:16— "For God so loved the world that he gave his one and only Son, that whoever believes in him shall not perish but have eternal life."

3. *Make a list of who should be notified of your passing.* It can be painful when people who were important in your life do not know of your death until after the funeral simply because nobody thought of letting them know. It will be helpful to your family if they have a list of agencies that need to be notified, such as Social Security, pension plans, IRA administrators, life insurance companies, clubs and fraternal organizations you belong to, or your home church. And don't forget to let your survivors know of any automatic withdrawals from your bank account and credit cards that need to be cancelled.

4. *Pass on a blessing.* A tourist was hospitalized on a trip to a Middle Eastern country. In the bed next to his was an elderly man who looked like a biblical patriarch.

It turned out he also acted like a patriarch from Bible times. As the tourist watched in amazement, he saw a crowd of relatives coming in to say farewell to the old man who was near death. Summoning his last strength, the man had every family member, young and old, approach the bed in turn. He placed his hand on each of them and pronounced a blessing appropriate to the individual. Deeply moved, the tourist contemplated what a wonderful gift such a blessing can be. A blessing does not have to be a ritual administered by clergy. A blessing is an affirmation, an encouragement, a focus on the future, a statement of faith that good will come to the one being blessed. Words of faith and love spoken by those nearing the end will be cherished for years to come.

5. *Be reconciled.* Forgiveness has been dealt with extensively in the first chapter. It is just mentioned here as a reminder that this is one important aspect of being concerned for the wellbeing of your survivors.

6. *Set your survivors free.* Charlene came to her pastor with a terrible dilemma. She told how five years ago her husband, Bruce, was terminally ill. Shortly before he died, he had asked her to promise that she would not marry again. "I could not get myself to say no to my dying husband," Charlene said, "so I made the promise.

Now I have met a man I love, and we want to get married. But I promised Bruce that I would not. What am I to do?" She also told how now she felt resentment against Bruce for having made an unreasonable request when she was emotionally vulnerable. The upshot of this pastoral consultation was that the pastor and Charlene agreed that Bruce under the stress of his own dying, had taken advantage of Charlene, and that she should both forgive him for that and also not feel bound by a promise made upon an invalid request. This story points to the fact that people who are dying must give their loved ones freedom to get on with their lives, wherever the uncertain future may lead. How much better Charlene's memory of Bruce would have been if he had released her to that freedom.

Ways to Show Love

How can we help one another when a loved one has passed on? We will not all have the same needs. Some in the family will have been closer to the departed one than others, so the intensity of grief will vary. It will be harder for people who are left alone than for those who are surrounded by family and friends. People also process grief differently; it may be much more painful for some than for others. People who want to care will keep their antennas up so they can be supportive where needed. Here are some reminders of how we may show our love.

1. *Be there for each other.* Two thousand years ago Jesus urged John and Mary to be there for each other. People still need that kind of support system. Support does not have to be complicated. The most important part of caring is being there for the other person. For example, suppose you ask someone how he is doing, and the response is, "Fine, I guess." Did you get the "I guess"? That's a red flag. It means he is really not fine. Don't just pass this person by, but give him an opening for saying more. You might respond with something like, "I bet you do have some difficult days—is this maybe one of them?" Or if the time is not right just then for more talk, give the other person a call later in the day.

   One relationship where we really need to be there for each other is in marriage. It is a tragic fact that many marriages do not long survive the death of a child. They break up because two people, who managed the business of living together fairly well, discovered that in their deep anguish they could not be there for each other. It is important to develop sensitivity to the unspoken needs of the partner. Imagine Jesus saying (as a paraphrase of what he said to Mary and

John), "Wife, here is your husband, and husband, here is your wife." Those who are partners in grief must find times to open up to each other. Someone needs to start the conversation by saying something like, "I am really hurting inside; how is it with you?" The worst thing you can do is say, "I can't talk about it; you will just have to deal with it yourself." If you cannot get the conversation going between the two of you, find a third party to help you with it.

And do not forget bereaved children. It takes time and patience to be supportive to them. Don't just ask them, "How are you doing?" They will probably shrug their shoulders and say, "Okay." And that ends the conversation. It is better to do something with them—if they are young, sit on the floor with them and participate in their play with their toys. After a while you might say something like, "I really miss your brother (or mother or friend), and it makes me feel sad." Let the words just hang for a while. Don't get nervous if there is silence. Eventually you might say, "What do you do with your sadness?" See what conversation might develop, and go with the flow. For older children, take them somewhere. The ride in the car is the best time to talk. Teens talk better with adults when they are next to each other, rather than face to face.

Whenever there is grief, there are Johns and Marys who need someone to be a mother or son (that is, a true soulmate) to them. If they are fortunate, they will have understanding and supportive family members, friends, or faith communities. Do make use of these natural support systems.

2. *Show deeds of kindness.* Bring a meal; offer to babysit; invite the bereaved one to a movie; help with household chores or yard work. An offer to help with sorting or disposing of the deceased one's clothing or tools or whatever may be very meaningful—just don't rush by trying to take care of it all in one bustling session. This is a time for giving the bereaved person a chance to reminisce and maybe tell stories. If at the end of the time nothing got done except conversation, it will have been time well spent.

3. *Find a group.* There are also organized resources, such as bereavement support groups, to help bereaved survivors negotiate the pains of grief. Most hospice organizations have support groups facilitated by one of their staff members. These groups are open to anyone in bereavement, even if the departed one was not under hospice care. Various churches and synagogues also sponsor bereavement support groups. Generally they also open their groups to anyone regardless of

religious affiliation. A good way to locate a support group in your community is to search online.

4. *Be aware of a survivor's financial needs.* Don't hesitate to ask—you are not prying; you are trying to help. If there are financial concerns, there may be agencies that provide help. If your community has a senior center, that may be a good resource for finding out what is available. Sometimes a financial gift from you might be just what is needed.

5. *Don't exclude the bereaved.* This is especially true for widowed people. Before the spouse died, they may have been in a social network of couples. All too often these networks ignore the single survivor. If you had fun with four or six people eating out together, commit to do it now with the uneven number.

This list is obviously not complete. Other ways of being supportive may come to mind. Always be ready to hear what the bereaved person is saying or hinting at. Don't judge anyone for grieving too much or too little. And if you don't know what to do, remember that the biggest part of helping is being there.

Prayer

Thank you, Jesus for showing us how to care.
We are all going through a difficult time. Help

us to be sensitive, not only to our own needs, but also to the pain of others. Help us especially to find comfort and strength in your love for us. I pray specifically for [name]: bring to my mind things that I can do to be of help. Amen.

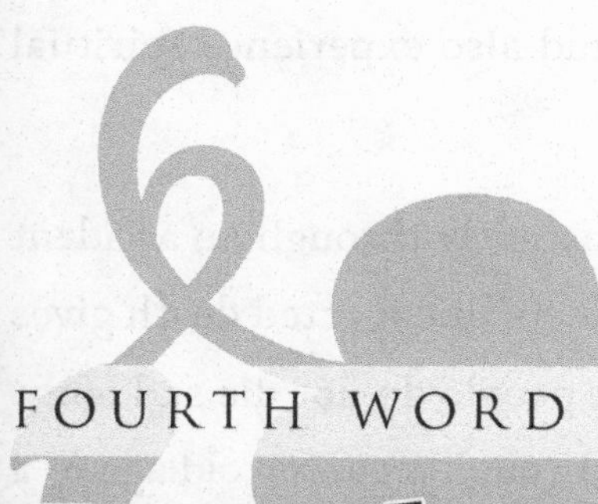

FOURTH WORD

Forsaken

> *At noon, darkness came over the whole land until three in the afternoon. And at three in the afternoon Jesus cried out in a loud voice, "Eloi, Eloi, lema sabachthani?" (which means "My God, my God, why have you forsaken me?") (Mark 15:33–34)*

The fourth word of the cross is a cry deep from the heart of Jesus. It is the cry of despair: "My God, my God, why have you forsaken me?"

It comes as a shock to see how Jesus—who, more than any other person, had lived his life in conscious harmony with God the Father—should now feel abandoned by the Father. If Jesus could feel God-forsaken, it is not surprising that many people near the end of life should also experience spiritual despair—God, where are you?

For some people, life may end instantly through an accident or a fatal heart attack. Their sudden, unexpected death gives no time for reflection. But most people do not die suddenly. For them the end comes either through creeping old age or a terminal illness. If this is our lot, there comes a time when we know we are in our last stage of life on this earth. Up to this point we may have lived with hope of healing. But eventually the facts pile up, and deep inside we sense and fear that we are dying. The road now leads us through a place where we have not been before, and where we do not choose to be.

This final road is the most traveled one. Every human being before us has traveled it. Yet we each experience it alone in a unique, personal way. It is not a straight, even road—we may experience wide mood swings ranging from peace to fear, from acceptance to rebellion, from hope to despair, from faith to doubt, from feeling loved to feeling forsaken.

And the stage of life we are in when we enter this final road makes a lot of difference. People suffering constant pain and discomfort may more readily welcome death. People in advanced old age may also express a preference for death rather than the indignities associated with losing control over mind and body. When people feel (often unnecessarily) that they have become a burden to their caregivers, they may also be more ready to accept the end of life. It is different for someone who is young, who has unfulfilled dreams of things yet to be done, who is leaving a spouse or young children. Peace and acceptance will be harder to come by in those situations.

Among the various feelings and emotions of the terminally ill, one that stands out is abandonment. The road to death may be the most traveled one, but at times it can also feel like the loneliest one. "My God, my God, why have you forsaken me?" cried Jesus for all the despairing.

Keeping Perspective

As we reflect on the fourth word, it is important that we keep our perspective—despair is not the overriding theme of the seven words of the cross. The first three and the last three words reveal that Jesus, in the midst of his own suffering, still cared for others and found peace for himself. But in between—there was the darkness.

In the same way, terminally ill people may face a crisis of faith. As we see in the case of Jesus, this crisis of faith is not the last word. He came through it, and so, by the grace of God, will we. But it should not shock us or our loved ones when despair closes in on us.

Scott had been a committed Christian all his life. His children saw him as a great dad and devout role model. He was respected in his profession as a man of integrity. He served in his community and church. His life was molded by his faith in Jesus. When he was diagnosed with a terminal illness, he maintained his strong faith all the way through the long ordeal of medical treatments. His last weeks were lived with the knowledge that there was no further treatment—his end was approaching. For most of these days he was at peace, sustained by his faith. But then one day during these last weeks he told his pastor, "I don't believe it anymore." He said that God seemed far away and all looked dark. His pastor took him by the hand and for a long time just sat there in quiet empathy. Eventually, the pastor said, "Scott, Jesus experienced this also, and he came through it. You will do the same, for God will not let you go." In subsequent conversations, the pastor saw Scott's faith return. A few days later, Scott passed peacefully into glory.

Despair Is Not Weakness

Despair is not a sign of spiritual weakness or unbelief. As it happened to Jesus, it can happen to the most devout believer. Don't feel you have to pretend it is not so. Don't suffer your crisis of faith in silence. Jesus himself cried out his despair in a loud voice.

The words Jesus used are a quote from the first verse of Psalm 22. The Psalms are a spiritual textbook about saying it like you feel it. They teach us that we do not need to filter our emotions so we will sound more pious than we are. If doubt or despair is where you are, say so. The fourth word shows that faith is not always upbeat. Yes, it can lead us to heights of joy, but faith may also plunge us into depths of anguish.

Faith is deeply personal. It is much more than a doctrine we have learned or traditions we cling to. Faith is our very relationship with God—who is unseen and whose ways are often inscrutable. Particularly in a time of crisis, our faith may become gritty. We might experience despair, yet we may also recognize seeds of hope. It is in this crucible that we learn what faith is all about. Faith is not the absence of doubt. Nor are despair and hope mutually exclusive. Jesus himself, in the depth of despair, still cried out to "my God"—he still expressed that relationship that only faith makes possible. As long as we can say, "My God," we can be assured that we will come through despair into renewed faith.

If you hear your loved one saying something like Scott said, do not panic or judge. People in a crisis of faith do not need lectures about unbelief. Nor do they need platitudes. What they need is heartfelt understanding. Out of that understanding we can gently point them to the fact that Jesus, after crying out his God-forsakenness, would in the end (as we will see in the sixth and seventh words) come to the triumphant faith of knowing that his task was done and he was in the hands of the loving Father in heaven.

A Lonely Road

It is clear from Jesus's Garden of Gethsemane experience that his anguish was a spiritual struggle. He had to accept that God his Father had laid out a terrible task for him. And perhaps his anguish was made even worse because he had no human support. Being attacked, misunderstood, or forsaken by people can easily translate into feeling forsaken by God as well. Jesus certainly experienced that.

He was the celebrity of his time, and crowds gathered to hear his every word, but there was one thing they did not want to hear him talk about—his impending death. His own disciples felt that Jesus would turn out to be the long-awaited Messiah. But in their way of thinking this meant that he would live a long and prosperous life. They envisioned for Jesus and themselves a future of power and glory. Therefore they never even tried to understand him when he opened his heart about the heavy task for which he was destined. They would not hear of his death.

Months before, Jesus had introduced his disciples to the fact that it was his destiny to be rejected and to die a sacrificial death. Led by Peter, his disciples vehemently rejected this prediction of suffering. Their denial was so strong that Jesus called it demonic (Matthew 16:21–23).

We see this particularly the night before his death when he was in the Garden of Gethsemane. Up to that point Jesus had faced his destiny and accepted it even though it weighed heavily on him. But now as the actual time was upon him, he experienced a deep inner struggle. He recoiled in fear and prayed, "Father, is there no other way? Please take this bitter cup from me." His agony was so great that his sweat became as blood.

Did his companions support and comfort him? Physically they were nearby, but instead of being supportive, they were asleep. Three times Jesus came to them and shared his anguish. He asked them to pray with him, but he received no support.

And so it was from Gethsemane onward. At his interrogations and trials, no witness for the defense came forward. When he could no longer carry the heavy cross, no sympathetic friend or admirer offered to do it for him. A stranger from Africa was drafted. Amid the jeering crowd Jesus stumbled alone to Calvary.

And then came the darkest moment when even God was not there. All his life Jesus had the most intimate sense of the nearness of God, whom he called his true Father. So close had been the bond that Jesus said he lived in the Father and the

Father lived in him (John 10:38). He had referred to that bond as the sustaining power of his life. Now that bond was broken. "My God, why have you forsaken me?"

The Climax of Suffering

In the series of the seven words, the fourth is the midpoint. That is significant. The fourth word marks the climax of suffering. In the first three words, Jesus was able to graciously forgive his enemies, encourage a fellow sufferer, and show concern for those who loved him. In the last two words, though still suffering greatly, Jesus came to peace and surrender. But in the fourth word we see Jesus shut out from any comfort. This is the worst; this is as bad as it gets.

There are two dimensions to Jesus's experience of being abandoned. The first is that he is so very different from us. Jesus is unique, and what happened in those three dark hours was unique to Jesus—yet it is of ultimate importance to all humanity. Jesus was, and is, at the core of his being, one with God the Father. As such he has existed since before the creation of the world. In coming to earth he became human in order to bring salvation to a lost human race. As savior he lived a life of love, taught people how to live, and brought healing wherever he went. The climax of his life came when he gave his life as a sacrifice for the sins of the world. In ways that are too deep for us to fully understand, this came to a head during three hours of darkness when all contact between him and his heavenly Father was severed. That is when he experienced the total despair of hell—being God-forsaken.

Because he, the Son of God, was forsaken by the Father, we need never fear that we will be forsaken by God. This is the heart of Christian faith—that because of the sacrificial death of Jesus, we are reconciled with God. Believe this, and through believing in Jesus find your peace with God. Even though someday you and I must die, we can trust that we will be forever with God. This is the good news Jesus wants the whole world to know. And this is also why the day he died is called Good Friday.

Forsaken by God

The second dimension to Jesus's experience of being abandoned is that he is so very much one of us. Though he existed eternally as Son of God, at his birth he also became Son of Man, which means he was fully human. Therefore what he experienced on earth is the common experience of humanity. The commonality between the experience of Jesus and what we may go through is that feeling God-forsaken can be the cumulative effect of major disappointments and other experiences of being forsaken. Serious illness hits hard with disappointment. Perhaps you lived a healthy lifestyle, and your parents lived to be in their nineties—why should you now be fighting serious cancer? It just does not seem fair. And when things don't seem fair, the implication behind it is, "My God, why have you forsaken me?"

You may also feel disappointed in the medical system. What happened to all the hopes you placed in modern medicine? You have gone through grueling medical protocols. You have been urged to fight. You had hopes when the surgery was "successful," or when you were in remission. But the disease came back, and now it all comes crashing down on you. We know that we cannot really blame the medical establishment. They gave it their best shot. Ultimately our deepest thought may be, *God, why did you not bless the medical treatments? Why did you let me down? Why have you forsaken me?*

There are people who in desperation turn to alternative medicine. Their regular doctors have told them there is nothing more that can be done. But the alternative medicine literature promises amazing results. So people buy expensive concoctions or visit foreign clinics. But in spite of all this, they are not getting better. Now they feel they have been scammed. It is another blow of feeling let down. "My God, I have tried everything—why have you forsaken me?"

Forsaken by People

We may also experience abandonment by people. People we had counted on as friends and family are now not coming to see us. Maybe they avoid us because they have never come to terms with their own mortality. They may even give the excuse that they cannot stand to see someone suffer. And of course, busy-ness can be a convenient excuse. Whatever the reason, people let us down when we need their love. Again we experience being forsaken.

Religious affiliation doesn't necessarily help either. Some Christian churches base a major part of their message and ministry on miraculous healing. "God does not want you to be ill," they teach. "God always answers prayer." You have heard it, believed it, and prayed it. Yes, how you have prayed! Others have prayed as well—friends and work associates have put your name on the prayer chains of their churches, and people you do not even know have prayed for you. But healing is not happening—maybe to others, but not to you.

It is particularly bad when people imply that if you had more faith, God would have healed you. Some churches that are heavily based on faith healing do not know how to fit the dying into their belief system, so they abandon their wounded. Church members and pastors quit visiting. "My God, why have you forsaken me?"

Feelings and Reality

But has God forsaken you? You may *feel* forsaken, but that is different from actually *being* forsaken. At the age of forty-two,

I had a medical disaster that brought me to the cusp of death. I was taken to the emergency room with massive internal bleeding. My blood loss was faster than transfusions could replenish it. I was in and out of awareness, but I remember at one point lying on a gurney with attendants literally running beside it through long hospital hallways as they rushed me into surgery. I knew that I was facing imminent death, and it was bleak and lonely.

I wish I could tell you that I saw the lights of glory beckoning me to heaven. But for me it was not like that. What I saw in my mind was an immense gray fog, like a wall, and I was moving toward it. There was nothing else—just me moving toward that grim wall of the unknown. I felt very alone and forsaken. In my heart I cried out, "Jesus, all my adult life I have preached and taught others about you, but now when I need you most, where are you?" Immediately another thought came to me and I prayed, "Jesus, you have gone through this wall of death; take me by my hand and lead me through." And with that a peace came over me, and I knew that I would be all right regardless of whether I lived or died.

The next thing I knew, I was coming out of anesthesia. Before I could even move my limbs, my mind was clear, and I recognized I was in the recovery room. I said to myself, "Well, I am still in this world. But if it had been otherwise, that would be okay too." The peace was still there.

Not Forsaken

Yes, Jesus the Son of God had gone through that wall of death. He too had experienced the anguish of being forsaken. And that has a direct bearing on us. He experienced it so that we would never really be forsaken. He went alone so that we would not have to go alone. In your heart and mind, reach out to him and ask him to take you by the hand. Know that even when you feel forsaken, you are not forsaken.

The words, "My God, my God, why have you forsaken me?" are from Psalm 22. The next Psalm, the beloved Psalm 23, is the counterpoint to this: "Even though I walk through the valley of the shadow of death, I will fear no evil; for you are with me; ... Surely your goodness and love will follow me all the days of my life, and I will dwell in the house of the Lord forever" (selections from Psalm 23).

Prayer

> God, sometimes I feel so alone. Does anybody really understand what I am going through? I am tired of disappointments. Sometimes I even wonder if you exist. But even in my darkest moments, I still resolve to call you my God. Dear God, my God, help me. Let me know that

> you are near. And let Jesus, who himself went through dark despair, take me by the hand and lead me through to the light. In his name I pray. Amen.

FIFTH WORD

Thirst

Later, knowing that everything had now been finished, and so that Scripture would be fulfilled, Jesus said, "I am thirsty." A jar of wine vinegar was there, so they soaked a sponge in it, put the sponge on a stalk of the hyssop plant, and lifted it to Jesus' lips. (John 19:28–29)

One day, while traveling through Samaria, Jesus met a woman at Jacob's well and asked her for a drink. From that simple request the conversation quickly evolved into a profound discussion about finding true fulfillment. This, Jesus said, does not come from religious ritual but from drinking the living water that he gives to those who are thirsting for it (John 4). Sometime later in the Jerusalem temple Jesus again used the term "living water" (John 7:38) to describe the spiritual empowerment people could receive through believing in him. And on a teaching trip in Galilee he declared, "Whoever believes in me will never be thirsty" (John 6:35). In each of these cases Jesus used the terms "living water" and "thirst" as metaphors to describe how he himself is the inexhaustible quencher of spiritual thirst.

But following the dark hours of God-forsakenness Jesus himself was drained dry—he was not thinking of water now as a figure of speech, but expressing a desperate physical need. Although for hours he had experienced terrible pain, the fifth word is the first time he speaks about his own physical suffering. Thus the fifth word leads us to think of the physical needs of the terminally ill. Exploring the implications of the fifth word can help both the patient and the caregivers.

Physical Pain

What was the condition of Jesus when he said, "I am thirsty"? If anything exemplifies the degradation to which human beings can sink, it was the invention and sadistic refinement of crucifixion. Crucifixion was practiced in several brutal ancient cultures, and particularly so on a large scale by the Romans. Without going into the gruesome details, we can say that it was designed to kill a person slowly and most painfully. One effect was that the blood loss, especially when crucifixion was preceded by flagellation, caused depletion of body fluids and hence extreme thirst. This, combined with the contorted position of the body, could cause unbearable cramps. Earlier Jesus had been offered a narcotic-laced potion of wine and myrrh (Mark 15:23). This concoction would dull the senses enough to alleviate some of the pain. It was probably offered to him by sympathetic followers. But in spite of his thirst, Jesus had refused it. It is generally believed that he refused it because he wanted to be fully alert to the end. But when the end was very near, he accepted a sip of the sour wine that was offered him on a sponge. This moistening of the mouth enabled him to utter the last two words from the cross in "a loud voice" (Luke 23:46).

Our need may, or may not be, as in the case of Jesus, a need for water. But there are needs at the end stage of life, and once again we see how in his dying hours Jesus shares the experience of those who suffer. He, who was the fountain of life from before time began, became human in every respect, including having a body that was critically dehydrated. In dying as well as in living, he speaks to us from experience.

Humiliation

Paintings of the crucifixion often show Jesus hanging naked on the cross, except for a discreet loincloth covering his private parts. In reality that loincloth was not there. Crucifixion was designed not only to cause greatest pain, but also to rob the condemned of all dignity. Onlookers were encouraged to mock, humiliate, and revile the naked victim.

Our end of life will be different from what Jesus went through. We live in a more humane society where people normally do not willfully inflict pain and humiliation on us. Yet, we too may experience both physical suffering and humiliation. In time our aging bodies develop limitations that can be painful and embarrassing. All this can be accentuated by various forms of illness.

It is humiliating when our mobility declines and we have to rely on walkers and wheelchairs to get around. It is humiliating when we can no longer feed ourselves, or if we still can, it may be messy. An even greater humiliation is incontinence, which subjects us to the need for others to clean and change us. Hopefully we will be cared for by family members and healthcare workers who love us and seek to minimize our embarrassment. But even kind caregivers may become exasperated when we need to be helped again and again. They may try to hide their frustration, but we will sense it and feel bad about being a burden to others.

For many, the greatest fear is dementia—the breakdown of the mind. Dementia sneaks up on us, moving from growing mental confusion to total social isolation and loss of physical functions. Dementia strikes randomly. My mother died from it at eighty-two, but my father's mind remained clear and he was able to live by himself in his own house until he died of heart failure at ninety-two. There appears to be no rhyme or reason as to who will be affected by dementia. Dementia is unpredictable, and that adds to its fearsomeness.

The question is how we will handle the disabilities, not only when they happen, but also when we worry that they may be our future. Will these things envelop us with fear, frustration, and barely concealed anger? Or can we trust that we are in the hands of a loving God? Can we believe that beyond our current difficulties there will be life in another dimension that we refer to as heaven? Coming to that peace may not be easy. It is one thing to sing of the joy of believing and the hope of glory when we are well. But when the body suffers, it gets our attention and can easily dominate all our awareness. Therefore this, more than ever, becomes a time to draw on the resources of our faith.

Beyond the Brokenness

There is currently in vogue in some churches and by various televangelists a teaching that God does not want us to be sick and suffering. We are told that if we have enough faith and the right attitude, our problems will disappear. That is not what Jesus taught. He was realistic about the fact that believers may face great difficulties, as he himself did. The faith taught by Jesus and handed down by the apostles is not about a walk through the rose garden of life. It honestly faces up to life in a broken world.

But faith looks beyond the brokenness to the love of God who will see us through. In the Old Testament there is a remarkable book called Lamentations. In powerful poetic language it describes the pain and humiliation suffered when Jerusalem was utterly destroyed in 586 BC. In the midst of this elegy of pain, faith breaks out in one of the most memorable verses in the Bible:

> Yet this I call to mind
> and therefore I have hope:
> Because of the Lord's great love we are not consumed,
> for his compassions never fail.
> They are new every morning;
> great is your faithfulness.
> I say to myself, "The Lord is my portion;
> therefore I will wait for him."
>
> (Lamentations 3:21–24)

A New Testament verse also speaks powerfully to this:

> Therefore we do not lose heart. Though outwardly we are wasting away, yet inwardly we are being renewed day by day. For our light and momentary troubles are achieving for us

> an eternal glory that far outweighs them all. So we fix our eyes not on what is seen, but on what is unseen, since what is seen is temporary, but what is unseen is eternal. (2 Corinthians 4:16–18)

The entire passage, which runs from 2 Corinthians 4:7 to 5:10, is worth reading and reflecting on. It describes how life in this world can at times be very difficult, as Jesus himself experienced. But if we have faith, we do not need to despair—God will not allow us to be defeated. There is an end to suffering and a new life to come.

Avoiding Mortality

There was a time when hardship and death were common experiences. I remember visiting an old graveyard where a family gravestone bore record of four young children who had died of disease all at separate dates within a period of six months. This was not unusual, and as a result, Christians thought and spoke much more often about a future hope that goes beyond this life. We are privileged to live in a time when such tragedies are rare. But has our more prosperous and secure life led us to avoid thinking about our mortality? Reality cannot be denied; death is universal—we all will die. For some the dying process will be easier than others. But regardless of how we pass on, let us consciously draw on the resources of faith, speak about them, and celebrate them. Then, in the time of need, we can encourage each other and ourselves with the assurance that Jesus too suffered—and he came through victoriously. His Word promises that as he did, so shall we, because of him (1 Corinthians 15:22).

Admitting Weakness

When Jesus was near death, the only help he received was a sponge filled with sour wine to moisten his parched mouth. Earlier, at the beginning of the crucifixion, Jesus had refused the wine and myrrh mixture. By this he indicated that he needed to be alert during what was to follow. But as we will see in the sixth word, his task is now completed, and he is ready to ask for a drink. This is an act of humility. Here we see the great thirst-quencher announcing his own need for a drink. He teaches an important aspect of dying well: are we willing to admit weakness and receive help?

I was speaking with a friend about end-of-life issues. He said, "When I am so helpless that I cannot feed myself and need people to change my diapers, I will commit suicide; I will not be humiliated, nor will I be a burden to others." I also tend to be a self-sufficient person, so I can understand the sentiment. For many of us it is hard to admit need and receive help, especially when that help relates to intimate personal matters. But Jesus models for us a humility that we should pay attention to. He gives us this fifth word to remind us not to be too proud to ask for help. In fact, the Bible specifically describes Jesus's death with the words, "He humbled himself" (Philippians 2:8).

Meekness and Mercy

In his Sermon on the Mount, Jesus said, "Blessed are the meek" and also "Blessed are the merciful." In the process of our dying, the needs of the meek and the work of the merciful meet together in the bond of love. When we are in extreme need we should not feel that we are a burden to those who love us. Let us be humble enough to receive what they are ready to give. Both giver and receiver will be blessed.

Not the End

Let us also keep in mind that our worn-out body is not the end of life's story. Three days after his death, Jesus appeared to his followers with a body that was transformed and more alive than ever. The Bible compares death with sowing a seed in the ground. The seedling that emerges is far greater than what was sown, and the same is true of our earthly bodies. This is how the apostle Paul describes it in his letter to his friends in Corinth:

> The body that is sown is perishable, it is raised imperishable; it is sown in dishonor, it is raised in glory; it is sown in weakness, it is raised in power; it is sown a natural body, it is raised a spiritual body. (1 Corinthians 15:42–44)

Prayer

> Dear Jesus, this is not an easy time for me. I am so helpless and so weary. Please encourage me. It is also a hard time for those who are helping me. Please bless them. And help us to be patient with each other. I know that this is only one stage in my existence. Help me to keep focused on the time when all this suffering is past and I will be with you and all your people in glory. Amen.

Addendum: On Care for the Terminally Ill

We live in a time when drugs and surgery can do amazing things to bring healing, relieve pain, and extend life. Consequently people place great hope in modern medicine. But medical treatment can go only so far. At some point—either because our aging bodies are just worn out, or because of the incurability of an illness—no amount of medical treatment can bring healing. Continuing with "heroic measures" may then cause more harm than good. For example, chemotherapy can make one very miserable. It is worth doing as long as there is hope that it will arrest or reverse the progression of the disease. But when it is no longer effective, we are better off without it. There is a point where stopping aggressive treatment can give us better quality of life for the remaining time we have. That is the time to give serious thought to hospice care.

Hospice is for people who, in the estimation of their doctors, have most likely less than six months of life expectancy. The purpose of hospice care is to make the final months of a person's life as comfortable as possible. The focus is on the quality of life for whatever time is remaining. This means ending aggressive treatments when they are no longer effective and may only cause more suffering. Instead, patients are given palliative care, which focuses on relieving pain and promoting comfort and dignity. Hospice also gives support to the patient's family members or other caregivers.

Entering hospice care requires the courageous realism of recognizing that the illness is terminal. Hospice does not hasten death. In fact, a 2007 study reported in the *Journal of Pain and Symptom Management* claimed that hospice patients live an average of twenty-nine days longer than similar patients without hospice care.[2] And entering hospice care does not mean signing your life away; it can be revoked at any time. Occasionally patients improve under hospice care to the extent that they can be discharged from hospice.

Hospice is not a facility to which patients are moved; it is a system of care. Though some hospice organizations have a hospice house to which a patient can be admitted, most hospice care is provided in the patient's own home. People who are living in a nursing home can receive hospice care in that nursing home in addition to the care they are already receiving from the facility staff. There are over four thousand hospice organizations in the United States, ranging from national corporations with thousands of patients to small local organizations. Whatever their size, they have to be accredited and maintain approved standards of care.

Upon admission each patient is assigned a care team consisting of a registered nurse (who is the leader of the team), a certified nurse assistant, a social worker, and a chaplain. This team regularly reports to a hospice physician. Some hospices also provide additional professional services, such as music therapy. The professional team is augmented by volunteers who provide companionship and housekeeping assistance.

---

[2] Stephen R. Connor, Bruce Pyenson, Kathryn Fitch, Carol Spence, and Kosuke Iwasaki. "Comparing Hospice and Nonhospice Survival Among Patients Who Die within a Three-Year Window." *Journal of Pain and Symptom Management* 33.3 (2007): 243.

In the United States, hospice care is generally funded by Medicare, or sometimes by other insurers.

Unfortunately, many people do not avail themselves of the care hospice can give. Often they wait till the very last days of life before turning to hospice. Thus they miss out on a lot of comfort that could have been given to them and their caregivers if they had enrolled earlier.

Why do people shy away from hospice care?

One reason is that they may be in denial. Death is a very hard thing to accept. It is the last thing we want to have happen to us, and so we keep hoping for a way out. But when hope goes against the evidence, we are setting ourselves up for disappointment and disillusionment. It takes courage to be realistic. But it is the best way. We are more likely to come to peace, and we may have a better quality of life when we accept the inevitable.

Another reason for avoiding hospice care is that people around us may discourage us from doing so. They may scold us for "giving up," or tell us to keep on fighting, or guilt us by saying, "We can't do without you." Sometimes they urge us to hang in as long as we can because a new medical discovery could be just around the corner. Their intentions may be good, but in almost all cases we would be better served by people who can gently help us face facts. The best way to love and help one another is in the real world.

People of religious faith may avoid hospice because they think that entering hospice care demonstrates lack of faith in God's power to heal. I certainly believe that God can heal anything at any time. But God also speaks to us through the events of life. And when all medical indications are that healing is not happening to us, our faith needs to begin focusing on the greater life that is drawing closer. Jesus himself died in great pain and torturous discomfort. But as we will see in the last two words of the cross, he died with faith and confidence in God. So for us, when all the signs are that God has another plan for us than healing, faith is expressed in surrendering to the will of God, and anticipating the life that is to come.

After serving forty-five years as a pastor, I thought I was retiring from active ministry. But God had other plans for me. I was asked by my friend, Ronke Adeyemi, to serve as chaplain in the Chicago hospice organization of which she was CEO. I accepted, and this opened a whole new perspective for me on the humane physical and spiritual care that is available to the terminally ill. But occasionally I also saw how uninformed people can undermine the hospice process.

One patient I attended to was a devout man of faith. After a long illness there came the time when his doctors told him there was nothing they could do anymore to bring healing or prolong life. As a Christian he accepted this with grace. He was at peace with God and not afraid to die. His two daughters, aided by the hospice staff, gave him the best of loving care in his own home. As the end came near, he withdrew more within himself (which is not unusual), spent most of the time sleeping, and quit eating. It was then, at the very end, that the oldest son flew in from out of state. He walked into the house as a man who knew all about being in control. When he heard that dad had not eaten for three days, he went into a rage and accused his sisters of starving his dad. He then called 911 and had the paramedics take his dad to the emergency room, where he insisted that the doctors put a feeding tube into his dad's stomach.

Before I continue with the story, let me make an important point. When a person nears death, it is common for the body to start shutting down. Urine output will often cease; the patient may go from hot to cold and back to hot again as the processes that maintain normal body temperature no longer function; usually breathing becomes erratic. So also the digestive system shuts down. The patient no longer feels hunger because the body is no longer able to process food. Forcing food into the body, whether by mouth or by feeding tube, will only cause discomfort created by a mess of undigested food in the stomach and intestines. That is why hospice staff will always tell caregivers to only give a patient food if the patient wants it. Never force it on a terminally ill patient. The rule is that people do not die because they are not eating; they are not eating because they are dying.

Now back to the above-mentioned story of the patient whose son took control: the emergency room doctor did put in the feeding tube. The patient was admitted to the hospital, where in strange surroundings he lived two more uncomfortable days before death ended his suffering. In effect, the son turned a peaceful dying-at-home process into a medical emergency that resulted in the very thing hospice seeks to avoid—invasive, useless medical procedures in a clinical setting that only cause discomfort to the patient.

The modern hospice movement dates back to the 1950s, when a British medical doctor, Dame Cicely Saunders, began focusing on the specific needs of the terminally ill. She developed the concepts of palliative care and dying with dignity. During the 1960s her ideas were introduced into the United States.

But the concept goes back to medieval times when monks and nuns in various Christian orders gave whatever relief they could to seriously ill patients. They did not have much in the way of effective medical treatment, but they gave loving care in the name of Jesus.

Jesus, who himself suffered so much, has been the greatest motivator in history for those who care for the sick and dying. While modern hospice is not a specifically religious movement, its spirit goes back to the sponge full of sour wine given to Jesus when he said, "I am thirsty."

SIXTH WORD

Finished

> *A jar of wine vinegar was there, so they soaked a sponge in it, put the sponge on a stalk of the hyssop plant, and lifted it to Jesus' lips. When he had received the drink, Jesus said, "It is finished." With that, he bowed his head and gave up his spirit.* (John 19:29–30)

When Jesus spoke the sixth word, "It is finished," he declared that his life's work was done. Actually, according to the gospels of Matthew and Mark, he did not just say it; he shouted it in a loud voice. This was no defeated sigh of resignation. It was a triumphant exclamation that he had completed what he came to do. There was no more to be added.

By the standards of this world, Jesus did not have much of a legacy to celebrate. When he died, it did not appear that he had made any difference to anybody. There was no more peace on earth than on the day he was born. He had brought no social change—the poor were still poor; his people were still oppressed by Roman rule; and his message of love had been drowned out in cries of "Crucify!" Jesus left not one written word. He invented nothing new. He was awarded no honors. Instead, he died in disgrace—condemned by both Jewish and Roman courts, forsaken by his followers, mocked by his enemies, and jeered by the populace. Yet, in the face of all this, he shouted triumphantly, "It is finished." He had done all that he was supposed to do. As he had said in a prayer just the previous evening, "[Father,] I have brought you glory on earth by finishing the work you gave me to do" (John 17:4).

As we approach the end of our earthly life, we also face our own "It is finished." We have come to the time when our earthly work is done. This does not just refer to work as our job or career. Our life's work includes what we have invested in relationships with friends and family. These interactions will now end. There are also things that will remain undone: uncompleted projects, vacation trips we were going to make, anticipation of a carefree retirement, old acquaintances we were planning to look up, and other unfulfilled dreams. If, at the end of our days, they have not yet been done, we realize that they will remain undone.

At that time we must be able to let go—to find peace with both what has been done and what has not been done. As to what has not been done, let us accept that some things we wanted to do really were not of ultimate importance. So, you never made that trip to a faraway exotic place—does it really matter? Facing death clarifies what is important and what is not.

What Is Important?

What then is truly important? The world's history books are filled with the names of the great and famous—presidents, kings, queens, generals, explorers, inventors, and artists. But what about ordinary people—do their lives matter? Yes, we can be assured that they do. In fact, when we come before God, we are all ordinary people. There is no special welcome and expedited processing for celebrities on judgment day. What will be remembered is how we expressed and lived our basic humanity, whether as CEO or bathroom-cleaner. Jesus said, "If anyone gives even a cup of cold water to one of these little ones who is my disciple, truly I tell you, that person will certainly not lose their reward" (Matthew 10:42). What counts in the end is what has been done in love.

Jesus himself is the model for that. As we noted above, on the day he died, it certainly did not look like he was headed for the history books. But from the perspective of two thousand years later, we know that his impact has been greater than that of any other human being. Even though he himself never went much beyond the boundaries of Judea and Galilee, he trained his disciples to spread his teachings to the ends of the earth. And what did he teach? By word and deed he revealed the love-nature of God in a way that had never been done before. He taught a way of life that is not self-centered but based on self-denial for the sake of others. He turned accepted values upside down when he declared that poor people and grieving people and humble people and others who are not the world's success stories will be especially blessed by God. He highlighted forgiveness of sinners and acceptance of outcasts. None of this has ever become the law of any country, but these teachings live in the hearts of millions and have inspired great deeds of service to humanity. However, all of this is subsidiary to, and derives from, the focal point of Jesus's life and death. We will consider that at the end of this chapter.

We also must realize, as we near the end of our lives, that even if there are no monuments to our achievements, our lives have had meaning. The good we have done will be remembered. We have done our part. And after we are gone, others will carry on. Life will go on without us, and that is okay.

Letting It Go

But what if we have failed? A man I will call Rudy spent the last weeks of his life in a nursing home. His family wanted nothing to do with him and did not visit him. If he ever had any friends, they did not show up either. When I as a chaplain visited him, he barely acknowledged my presence and would not enter into any conversation with me. But there was a nurse whom Rudy trusted. One day he said to her, "I have lived a rotten life and have never done any good to anybody."

What could she say to that? She took his hand and said, "Rudy, that is all past now; you must let it go. The one thing you must now hold on to is that God forgives and God loves you. Put your trust in Him."

Yes, when we come to the end we have to let it all go—the good and the bad. Hard though it may be, that is what we need to come to—acceptance and surrender to the will of God. Our faith now must be that God will provide for those we leave behind, that others will complete our unfinished tasks, that life will go on without us. This is big. Our aspirations and our fears fight against it. But faith wins out, and after stress and struggle, we are able to let it go. When we come to that point, we too have successfully completed our journey of faith, and we can say, "It is finished."

When the Time Comes

But we do not all come to the finish at the same stage of life. It is one thing to let go when you have lived a long life, accomplished various things, and now have no one who depends on you. Maybe you have not done all you wanted to do, but you can accept that. For people who are suffering, it may even be a relief to know that soon it will be finished.

It is not so easy when you have a family with young children or when you are engaged to be married. Or what about people who have dreams of doing humanitarian work? These things are important, and it is very difficult to let them go.

When I was a child, there was a woman in our town who felt God's call to do medical work in a third-world country. She went to medical school, and after passing her boards, she booked passage on a ship that would take her to her destination. On the way to the boat, she was struck by a street car and died instantly. Was all her dedication and preparation now a waste? Could it be said in any way that her task was finished? As a child I could not understand how God could allow this to happen to someone who was just ready to do God's work, and now, a lifetime later, I still cannot understand it.

We could ask the same about Jesus. Why did he have to die at about thirty-five years of age? Think of all the people he could have healed and all the things he could have taught if he had lived to be eighty. How much good could he have done if he had had more time? Wouldn't it be great if, at the end of a long life, he could have written his memoirs and other books to clarify his teachings? It was not to be that way. He knew that his time had come, and he accepted that as his Father's will. But as the Garden of Gethsemane scene shows, that acceptance did not come to him without a struggle. He literally sweated blood over it. Yet at the end of his struggle, he surrendered to his Father's will and had peace with it.

How can we come to such surrender and peace at the end of our lives? For that we need to understand and accept Jesus's "It is finished" at its deepest and most comprehensive meaning. Let us examine the sequence in which he spoke the last words of the cross and what happened in another nearby place while he said them.

The Complete Picture

We derive the seven words of the cross from the four gospels (Matthew, Mark, Luke, and John). They do not all tell us the same things, just like four different witnesses of an event would not relate identical stories. So too each one of the gospel writers presents and interprets what he saw or heard from a different perspective. By piecing these different observations together, we get a more complete picture of what really happened at Jesus's crucifixion.

Three of the four gospels tell us that just before he died, Jesus cried out in a loud voice. Matthew and Mark report the loud cry but do not say what Jesus said. John does not refer to the loudness of the cry but tells us the actual words: "It is finished." Luke adds to this what we call the seventh word: "Father, into your hands I commit my spirit." It appears likely that the sixth and the seventh words were spoken in quick succession, almost without pause.

Significantly, Matthew and Mark (who report the cry but do not give the words) tell us that as Jesus cried out, the curtain of the temple was torn from top to bottom. So there is a clear connection between the sixth word and the torn temple curtain. What is this connection?

The curtain of the Jerusalem temple divided the temple sanctuary into two parts. The first part was called the Holy Place. This was where the priests carried out their daily rituals. What happened there has some similarity to what takes place in churches—prayers (symbolized by incense) were offered; a grand menorah to give light to the place was tended every day (churches now use candles with the same symbolic meaning); and loaves of bread were displayed as a thanksgiving offering (just as now we express our thanks through financial offerings). All this temple action was carried out every day in the Holy Place.

The second part of the temple sanctuary was called the Most Holy Place. In this room there was no light and no action. It was as if time stood still. This represented the place where the timeless, eternal God dwelt. Because God is perfectly holy, no sinful human being was allowed to enter that place. But there was one exception—once a year on the Day of Atonement the High Priest entered this mysterious place to make atonement for the sins of the people. The prohibition against others entering the Most Holy Place was so strong that when the High Priest went behind that curtain, he had a trailing cord tied to his leg so people on the other side of the curtain could pull his body back out in case he fainted or had a heart attack. The massive curtain that separated the two parts of the temple symbolized the division between fallible human beings and our perfect, holy God. Sin makes us incompatible with God. This estrangement is the source of all our troubles and keeps us from ever finding total happiness.

Barrier Removed

Jesus came into this world to remove that barrier between God and us. He did that by offering his own life as atonement for sin. That is what he did when he submitted to the crucifixion. And when he had completed his mission, the curtain of separation was no longer needed. The miraculous tearing of the temple curtain testifies that God accepted Jesus's sacrifice. There is now no longer an impenetrable barrier between God and us. Truly Jesus could cry, "It is finished." He had done what he came to do.

This is of great significance for us as we contemplate the end of our earthly journey. It is not a time to dwell on our failures; nor is it a time to take pride in our achievements. It is a time to be humble—to realize that we are sinners.

Jesus came to save sinners. Because of Jesus, we can come into the presence of God without fear or shame. This is very clearly spelled out in the biblical book of Hebrews:

> Therefore, brothers and sisters, since we have confidence to enter the Most Holy Place by the blood of Jesus, by a new and living way opened for us through the curtain, that is, his body, and since we have a great priest over the house of God, let us draw near to God with a sincere heart and with the full assurance that faith brings, having our hearts sprinkled to cleanse us from a guilty conscience and having our bodies washed with pure water. (Hebrews 10:19–22)

Yes, we can come into the presence of God. Embrace that fact. Put your trust in the work that Jesus finished on your behalf. As you anticipate coming before God, come in faith and with your conscience cleansed because Jesus has cleared the way.

Any barrier between you and God has been removed—*it is finished.*

Prayer

> God, as I think back on what I have done with my life, I thank you for the good you enabled me to do. As for what I have done wrong, I now trust in your forgiveness. Most of all, heavenly Father, I thank you that regardless of my achievements or failures I may come into your presence without fear because Jesus completed his work of reconciliation. I pray in his name. Amen.

SEVENTH WORD

Commit

Jesus called out with a loud voice, "Father, into your hands I commit my spirit." When he had said this, he breathed his last. (Luke 23:46)

It may seem that with the seventh word we have come to the final moments of Jesus's life. But in reality, it was not at all final. When Jesus committed his spirit into the hands of God, he clearly signaled that he was not about to go into nothingness—he was going to his Father in heaven. The seventh word therefore is a word of transition—from time to eternity, and from the anguish of Good Friday to Easter celebration.

When people know the real meaning of Easter, they celebrate it with great joy. Forget about eggs and bunnies and daffodils—Easter is infinitely bigger than all that. It is the day of Jesus's resurrection. Easter is victory over death. It is the conviction that we are never at a dead end; no matter how bad things look, there is a way out. When we understand and believe the true Easter story, our lives are filled with joy—not because we experience a good day, but because we are headed for a good eternity.

A "Resurrection Culture"

I am indebted to Rob Moll, who in his excellent book, *The Art of Dying*, uses the term "the culture of resurrection." Rob argues in his book[3] that churches need to inculcate a culture of resurrection. This means that when we believe in the resurrection of Jesus, we will anticipate the future joyfully. We will dare to embrace death because it is followed by new life. And we will trust that even in this present life, good will come out of bad circumstances.

With a culture of resurrection, Christians in the early years of the faith faced death in the arena with courage and joyful anticipation of the life to come. That same spirit still lives today among believers around the world who suffer persecution. We too, when living out of a resurrection perspective, can find transforming power to deal with crisis and loss. As Paul the

---

[3] Rob Moll, *The Art of Dying: Living Fully into the Life to Come* (Downers Grove, IL: Intervarsity Press, 2010), 159ff.

apostle wrote: "We are hard pressed on every side, but not crushed; perplexed, but not in despair; persecuted, but not abandoned; struck down, but not destroyed" (2 Corinthians 4:8–9). Living in a culture of resurrection will give us hope at all times. The resurrection helps us see that even the ugly things of life can become a meaningful part of our journey.

It is good for us to have resurrection in mind as we come to terms with all the implications of the seventh word. Jesus spoke the seventh word at the moment of his dying. And that is the hard reality we all still have to deal with. As Jesus died, so each of us will leave this life through death.

Transition

The actual moment of death is a sacred time. I have served forty-five years as a pastor and six years as a hospice chaplain. During all those years, I have been present at many deaths. It never became routine for me. Each time again I was impressed with the immensity of the moment when the last breath was taken, the heart stopped, and the graph on the monitor went flat. A human being of infinite worth had transitioned from this temporal life into eternity.

How did Jesus make this transition? During his life Jesus had predicted that he would be put to death by the authorities, and then after three days rise again (Mark 8:31). Understanding that his death was ordained for a good purpose did not make dying easy for Jesus. Even believing that he would rise again did not make dying easy. Jesus struggled with it—first in the Garden of Gethsemane, and then while hanging on the cross as he went through three hours of despair. The fact that dying was a struggle even for Jesus, who had demonstrated faith enough to raise others from death, tells us that dying is a dreadful thing.

As we approach the end of life, we may experience feelings of dread. This may happen days or even just hours before the actual time comes. That is how it was in the case of Jesus. But when he came to the very end, fear and despair were left behind, and faith came through in full strength. He died in peaceful surrender with the seventh word on his lips. When my time comes, I hope to die like that.

God the Father

The seventh word, which actually was a phrase of several words, was not original with Jesus. He took it from Psalm 31:5. But he made an important addition to it. Psalm 31 says, "Into your [meaning God's] hands I commit my spirit." Jesus added the word *Father*. He made the phrase uniquely personal. Jesus often spoke of God as his Father. He also taught his disciples to think of God as their Father. The four gospels record 175 times in which Jesus spoke of God as Father. This intimate way of relating to God was original with Jesus. Before his time, in the Old Testament, there were some references to God as Father, but these were references to God as the Father of the nation of Israel. There is no evidence in the Bible that before Jesus anybody addressed God in a personal way as her or his Father. God was considered to be too holy and too great for an intimate personal relationship. In fact, traditionalists were so offended by Jesus calling God his own Father that they wanted to kill him for it (John 5:18).

As a result of Jesus's teaching it is now common to pray to God as "Father." With his teaching and his sacrifice on Calvary, Jesus has erased the intimidating gulf between God and us. This is very relevant for us in our time when we may feel insignificant in relation to the immensity of God. Today we know about the vastness and complexity of the universe, where time and distances are measured in millions of light years. If people believe in God at all, they are more likely to think of God as a force or energy permeating the universe. "Can such a cosmic force really be interested in me?" they might wonder.

Jesus says, "Yes, think of God as your loving Father." God is not an impersonal force. God knows your name; God understands you; God empathizes with you in your troubles and celebrates with you in your happiness.

There are people who have difficulty thinking of God as a father. They may have had bad experiences with dysfunctional fathers. But certainly Jesus was not thinking of that kind of father; to him the Father was perfect goodness personified. Sometimes people wonder why God should be called Father rather than Mother. We could say God is both, and God is neither. Everything we say about God is symbolic. That is the only way we can think about the infinite God who is pure spirit. Jesus chose to call God "Father." He derived his inspiration, strength and vision from his loving Father. We would do well to emulate him. Trust in God as the best of all fathers.

Trust and Preparation

And so we see how in his final words Jesus reaches out to the Father who loved him. The fear he experienced in Gethsemane and the despair of forsakenness are now behind. Jesus is at peace. In full trust and faith he commits his spirit into the hands of the Father. His example is an encouragement for us to seek to die like Jesus.

Like any good achievement, this is more likely to happen when we have prepared for it.

Preparing for death—is that possible? Is it desirable? People may dismiss this as a morbid preoccupation. We would rather avoid thinking about death, and we don't want to talk about it.

I once visited a church member in the cancer ward of a large hospital where he had received radiation for aggressive cancer. The treatment had not been successful, and the doctors said there was nothing more they could do for him. I found him nervous and restless.

I asked him, "How are you doing?"

He replied, "Well, I don't know, they are still doing tests to find out what is wrong with me."

I was a young, inexperienced preacher and did not know what to say. And unfortunately, because he was in denial, he did not give me a chance to speak with him about applying faith to his condition of being close to death and obviously very afraid. He died unprepared two days later. I am not saying that he is lost because we did not have a conversation about facing death. But his dying could have been more hope-filled and peaceful if he had accepted the reality of his condition and applied the comfort of his Christian faith.

There was a time when preparation for death was considered to be an important part of spiritual growth. From the middle ages through the Victorian era, books on the art of dying were popular. Pastors preached about it. And people had firsthand exposure to death when, as frequently happened, their loved ones died at home in the presence of extended family and neighbors. How things have changed! Most churchgoers would not welcome a sermon on dying. It is considered bad form to talk to even terminally ill people about death for fear that it might make them anxious or sad. And even near the end of life, people grasp at medical straws in hope of just a few more days. Why would a Christian be so averse to contemplating death? The Christian religion is built on the hope of an eternal life that is truly life to the full.

From This Life to the Next

To be sure, the only life we have experience with is this earthly life, and we value every day of it as a gift from God. But God has more in store for us. And when it appears that our days here are coming to an end, let us embrace with anticipation the joy of the life to come.

How can we prepare for dying well? A good starting point is to be realistic. When you are seriously ill, you can hope and pray for healing far into the illness. But there comes a time when you know in your heart that you are not going to be healed. This may be very depressing at first. But it is important to face up to it—please do not be in denial. Stuffing your feelings inside will not make it easier; this will only increase anxiety.

If you are a person of faith, this is the time to draw on the resources of your faith. If you have not been particularly religious, explore now the real meaning of the life, teachings, death, and resurrection of Jesus. It is not really all that complicated. It comes down to this verse: "Whoever believes in him shall not perish but have eternal life" (John 3:16).

Preparing and Sharing

Part of preparing is sharing. Let your loved ones know that you have accepted that you will not get better. Tell them you are ready to go to your heavenly Father. Some of them will tell you that you should not think that way but must keep believing that you will be healed. They also need to be realistic. If they will prepare themselves for the fact that there will soon be a parting, it will make their loss easier to bear when the time comes. It will also add value to the remaining time if patient and caregivers can all focus and talk about the hope that derives from the death and resurrection of Jesus.

Comforting Promises

There are some wonderful Bible passages that can help us and our loved ones during this time:

- Psalm 23 talks about going through the valley of the shadow of death without fear, and ending up in God's house forever.
- 1 Corinthians 15 is about Jesus's resurrection being the heart of Christian belief, and it describes what we may expect concerning our resurrection.

- Physical decline turning into eternal glory is concisely described in 2 Corinthians 4:16–18.
- In 2 Timothy 4:6–8 the apostle Paul writes how at the end of his life he anticipates receiving a "crown of righteousness" in the life to come.
- And John 14:1–6 relates Jesus's promise that there is lots of room in his Father's house, and he tells us how we can get there.

These passages are great to read and meditate on. Better yet, have someone else read them to you, and then discuss the verses together. And don't overlook Jesus's own last words: "Father, into your hands I commit my spirit."

Spirit and Soul

When we come to the end of earthly life our spirit is all we have left. Our possessions we cannot take with us; from our loved ones we must for now part; even the body is giving out. All that is left is our spirit. But that is really all that matters, for your spirit is you—indestructible, eternity-infused you.

The word *spirit* can be used interchangeably with the word *soul*. The spirit/soul is the essence of who you are. It includes your personality, your experiences, and your aspirations. It also includes something that you have never yet been—the perfection of yourself. All our lives we have been part of a sin-fallen world that kept us from being all that we were meant to be. This broken world will soon be left behind. The spirit goes to the Father. And when we get there, all that we are created to be will, for the first time, come into full bloom. When we meet our loved ones there, we will look at each other and say, "Wow, I never knew just how wonderful you are." Yes, when we commit ourselves to the Father, our spirits are in good hands, and the Father will complete what he intended us to be.

Eternity in Our Hearts

Actually, even in the midst of this fallen world, God has not left us totally in the dark about what is to come. The knowledge of eternity is really in our hearts. If only we would pay attention, we would recognize it. God has given us beauty as a signpost pointing to eternity while at the same time it draws attention to our mortality.

Sometimes it happens that when we experience something of exquisite beauty, we are overwhelmed with happiness and yet at the same time have a feeling of sadness because the full absorption of beauty seems to be beyond us. I believe that is what Ecclesiastes 3:10–11 points to: "I have seen the burden God has laid on the human race. He has made everything beautiful in its time. He has also set eternity in the human heart; yet no one can fathom what God has done from beginning to end." That haunting feeling of sadness is called a burden because it makes us aware of our limitation. But it is also a suggestion of hope because it makes us feel in our happiest moments that we are made for something even more than this.

Yes, God has put eternity in our hearts. People may argue as to whether there is a life after death. But no argument, no logic, no observation will prove or disprove eternal life. The answer is in our hearts. There is in our innermost self a longing for something that no earthly experience can ever satisfy. That innermost self can be referred to as heart or soul or spirit. And that is what in his last moment Jesus entrusted to the Father. "Father, into your hands I commit my spirit."

Greater Glory

I once visited a member of my congregation whom I will call Harry. His hobby was gardening, and the yard around his house was a riot of flowers. He even had a small orchard behind his house. The day of my visit was a perfect spring day. We walked out into his orchard, where the trees were in full bloom. Standing among this beauty, our conversation turned to heaven. We agreed that even though it was hard to imagine anything more beautiful than this spring day, heaven would exceed it by far. Harry said that he was ready to go there.

A few months after that visit, Harry became ill. It soon became obvious that this was a very serious illness. Harry underwent various courses of treatment, but nothing helped. His illness was terminal. I saw him waste away. About a year after our conversation in the orchard, I made my last visit to him. Again it was a beautiful spring day, nature showing all its glory, but for us there was now no orchard to delight in. Harry was in a hospital. I found him lying in bed and unresponsive. I tried to speak to him, but there was no reaction. So I took his hand in mine and stood that way by his bedside for a long time looking at his emaciated body and thinking back to that day a year ago when the world was so beautiful and life seemed good and he was in the best of health. For some reason, I don't know why, I involuntarily squeezed his hand, and to my amazement, he squeezed back. He then opened his eyes ever so slightly and looked at me. I smiled at him, and he, almost imperceptibly, nodded his head. Then his eyes closed again. There was no further response from him. But I understood. That slight nod of the head was an affirmation of the faith we shared. I stayed for a while, prayed for him, and then left. When, half an hour later, I arrived back at my office, there was a phone message that Harry had passed away at 11:45 a.m. And I realized that at the very moment I walked from the hospital lobby into a beautiful spring day, Harry had left the hospital to enter a far greater glory.

Jesus's last word is about trust: "Father, into your hands I commit my spirit." In the Bible, faith and trust are the same concept. We still use those words interchangeably. When you trust someone, you have faith in that person. Faith is trust, and trust is faith. Jesus died as he had lived, and as he had taught us to live.

Believe that your heavenly Father loves you; put your faith in this Father.

For many years, my wife and I have believed that God is our loving Father. When we had hard times, trusting in our Father got us through. The Father has provided for our needs. Ultimately though, it is not just about how the Father saw to it that we had food and clothing and could pay the bills. It is how the Father desires for us to be with Him in glory forever. That is why we believe that the greatest thing the Father has provided for us is the gift of his Son, Jesus. It is through Jesus that our sins are forgiven, and it is through Jesus that we too may come to the Father to enjoy eternal glory.

PRAYER

> *Father, into your hands I commit my spirit. In Jesus's name, amen.*

SELECT BIBLIOGRAPHY

Dolan, Susan and Vizzard, Audrey. *The End of Life Advisor: Personal, Legal, and Medical Considerations for a Peaceful, Dignified Death*. New York: Kaplan Publishing, 2009.

Fanestil, John. *Mrs. Hunter's Happy Death: Lessons on Living from People Preparing to Die*. New York: Doubleday, 2006.

Gawande, Atul, *Being Mortal: Medicine and What Matters in the End*. New York: Picador, 2014

Martin, James, SJ. *Seven Last Words: An Invitation to a Deeper Friendship with Jesus*. New York: Harper Collins, 2016.

Moll, Rob. *The Art of Dying: Living Fully into the Life to Come*. Downers Grove, IL: IVP Books, 2010.

Neuhaus, Richard John. *Death on a Friday Afternoon: Meditations on the Last Words of Jesus from the Cross*. New York: Basic Books, 2000.

Pink, Arthur W. *The Seven Sayings of the Savior on the Cross.* Grand Rapids, MI: Baker Books, 1984.

Verhey, Allen. *The Christian Art of Dying: Learning from Jesus.* Grand Rapids, MI: William B. Eerdmans Publishing Company, 2011.

Printed in the United States
By Bookmasters